All About Mount Fuji: A Kid's Guide to Japan's Sacred Mountain

Educational Books For Kids, Volume 30

Shah Rukh

Published by Shah Rukh, 2024.

ALL ABOUT MOUNT FUJI: A KID'S GUIDE TO JAPAN'S SACRED MOUNTAIN

First edition. October 14, 2024.

Copyright © 2024 Shah Rukh.

ISBN: 979-8224616510

Written by Shah Rukh.

Table of Contents

Prologue...1

Chapter 1: The Origins of Mount Fuji 2

Chapter 2: The Mystery of Fuji's Last Eruption 5

Chapter 3: Wildlife Around Mount Fuji 9

Chapter 4: Exploring Fuji's Five Lakes.........................14

Chapter 5: The Samurai Legends of Mount Fuji 19

Chapter 6: Climbing Mount Fuji: A Tradition 24

Chapter 7: The Ancient Shrines of Fuji 29

Chapter 8: Fuji in Japanese Art and Culture 34

Chapter 9: The Sacred Festivals of Mount Fuji 39

Chapter 10: Weather Wonders at the Summit................44

Chapter 11: How Mount Fuji Became a UNESCO Site 48

Chapter 12: The Forest at Fuji's Base.............................52

Chapter 13: Volcanic Secrets Beneath Mount Fuji 56

Chapter 14: Mount Fuji in Famous Japanese Stories....61

Chapter 15: Mount Fuji's Role in Modern Japan 66

Chapter 16: The Geology Behind Mount Fuji's Formation..........71

Chapter 17: Famous Explorers of Mount Fuji 76

Chapter 18: The First People to Climb Mount Fuji 81

Chapter 19: How Mount Fuji Inspires Creativity..........85

Chapter 20: Fun Facts About Mount Fuji and Beyond 90

Epilogue..95

Prologue

Welcome to the amazing world of Mount Fuji, Japan's most iconic and sacred mountain! Towering over the land with its perfect snowy peak, Mount Fuji is not just any mountain—it's a symbol of beauty, mystery, and adventure. For centuries, people have been mesmerized by its majesty, from ancient artists and poets to explorers and climbers.

In this book, you'll get to know Mount Fuji like never before. We'll take you on a journey through its fascinating history, its connection to Japanese culture and traditions, and the natural wonders that surround it. Have you ever wondered what makes Mount Fuji a volcano? Or why people climb it every summer? And what about the legends that say spirits live on its slopes? We'll answer all these questions and more!

Whether you dream of hiking to the summit or simply want to learn about the wildlife and plants that call this mountain home, you're in the right place. Get ready to uncover the secrets of Mount Fuji, from its fiery beginnings to the awe-inspiring views that have inspired countless visitors.

So, lace up your boots, grab your explorer's hat, and let's begin this exciting adventure together—because there's so much to discover about Japan's sacred mountain!

Chapter 1: The Origins of Mount Fuji

Mount Fuji, the tallest mountain in Japan, wasn't always the majestic, snow-capped peak we see today. In fact, it has a fascinating origin story that stretches back millions of years. Long before there were any people living in Japan, the land was shaped by powerful natural forces. Earthquakes shook the ground, and volcanoes erupted, spewing lava and ash. Mount Fuji is actually a volcano, which means it was created by molten rock, or magma, that came up from deep inside the Earth. When magma reaches the surface, it's called lava, and over many eruptions, layers of this lava built up, forming what would eventually become Mount Fuji.

But here's where things get interesting—Mount Fuji wasn't formed all at once. It actually has three distinct stages of development. The first stage started about 700,000 years ago. This is when the oldest part of the mountain, known as Komitake Fuji, began to form. Back then, the mountain was much smaller, and it didn't look like the grand peak we know today. The volcano would erupt, and lava would flow down its sides, slowly adding more material to the growing mountain. Komitake Fuji eventually went dormant, meaning it stopped erupting, but the story of Mount Fuji was far from over.

The second stage of Mount Fuji's development came around 100,000 years ago. This stage is known as Ko Fuji, which means "Old Fuji." During this time, the volcano became more active again, and a second layer of lava and ash was added on top of Komitake Fuji. The eruptions were often very powerful, and the mountain grew taller and steeper. However, Ko Fuji was still not the final form of Mount Fuji. Over thousands of years, the volcano's activity slowed down again, and for a while, it seemed like the mountain might have reached its final shape. But then came the third and most important stage—the formation of what we now call "New Fuji," or Shin Fuji.

The third and final stage began around 10,000 years ago. This is when Mount Fuji took on its iconic shape. Shin Fuji, or "New Fuji," grew even taller and wider than the previous stages, eventually reaching its current height of about 12,389 feet (3,776 meters). The eruptions during this time were massive, and the lava flowed down the sides of the mountain, creating smooth slopes that give Mount Fuji its symmetrical appearance. This stage of development was so dramatic that it covered most of the earlier Komitake and Ko Fuji volcanoes, so today, when you look at Mount Fuji, you're mostly seeing Shin Fuji.

What's amazing is that Mount Fuji is still considered an active volcano, even though its last eruption was over 300 years ago in 1707. That eruption, known as the Hoei Eruption, was so powerful that it left a large crater on the southeastern side of the mountain, and ash from the eruption even reached as far as the city of Edo, which is now known as Tokyo. Even though it hasn't erupted since then, scientists continue to monitor Mount Fuji closely because, like all volcanoes, it could erupt again someday.

Another interesting thing about the origins of Mount Fuji is that it is a "stratovolcano." This means that it is made up of layers, or "strata," of hardened lava, ash, and rocks. Each time the volcano erupted, new layers were added, making the mountain bigger and changing its shape. Over time, these layers built up into the tall, cone-shaped mountain that has become one of Japan's most famous landmarks.

The origins of Mount Fuji are not just about volcanic eruptions, though. The mountain also has deep roots in Japanese culture and mythology. According to one legend, Mount Fuji was created in a single night. The story goes that a woodsman named Visu woke up one morning to find that a huge mountain had appeared overnight in the field where he lived. The mountain, which was named Fuji, was said to be a gift from the gods. There are many other stories and legends that explain the origins of Mount Fuji, and these tales have been passed down for generations, becoming a part of Japan's rich cultural history.

In addition to its geological origins, Mount Fuji's name has an interesting history. The name "Fuji" is believed to come from an ancient Ainu word, "fuchi," which means "fire." The Ainu are an indigenous people who lived in Japan long before the modern Japanese culture developed. They saw Mount Fuji as a sacred place, and they believed that it was home to a powerful fire goddess. This connection to fire makes sense, given that Mount Fuji is a volcano that has erupted many times throughout history. However, some people believe that the name Fuji could also mean "immortal" or "everlasting," which fits perfectly with the mountain's long and enduring presence.

Mount Fuji's origins are not only geological and cultural but also spiritual. For centuries, people in Japan have considered the mountain to be a sacred place. In ancient times, it was believed that gods and spirits lived on the mountain, and it became a site of pilgrimage for those seeking spiritual enlightenment. Even today, thousands of people climb Mount Fuji each year, not just for the physical challenge but also for the spiritual experience of standing at the top of Japan's most sacred mountain. The origins of Mount Fuji are deeply connected to Japan's history, culture, and beliefs, making it much more than just a mountain—it's a symbol of the country's identity.

So, when you think about Mount Fuji, remember that it's not just a pretty mountain with a perfect shape. It's the result of millions of years of natural forces, volcanic eruptions, and layers of lava and ash. It's also a place filled with stories, myths, and spiritual significance that have shaped the way people in Japan view the world around them. From its humble beginnings as a small volcano to its towering presence today, Mount Fuji's origins are a reminder of the incredible power of nature and the deep connections between the land and the people who live there.

Chapter 2: The Mystery of Fuji's Last Eruption

Mount Fuji's last eruption, known as the Hoei Eruption, is one of the most mysterious and fascinating events in Japan's history. It took place over 300 years ago, in December 1707, but even today, scientists and historians are still trying to fully understand everything that happened during this dramatic event. The eruption lasted for about two weeks, and it had a huge impact not only on the mountain itself but also on the people who lived nearby. The eruption sent clouds of ash and smoke high into the sky, and it even reached the city of Edo, which is now called Tokyo, covering the area in a thick layer of volcanic ash. But what makes the Hoei Eruption so mysterious is that it wasn't exactly what people expected from a volcano like Mount Fuji.

First of all, Mount Fuji didn't erupt in the way that you might imagine when you think of a volcano. Most people picture lava flowing down the sides of the mountain, like a glowing river of molten rock. But during the Hoei Eruption, something different happened. Instead of lava pouring out, Mount Fuji mostly erupted ash, smoke, and small rocks known as volcanic debris. These materials were blasted into the air and spread across the surrounding areas, creating huge ash clouds that darkened the skies for miles around. The amount of ash was so great that it caused roofs to collapse under its weight, and crops were destroyed because they were covered by thick layers of ash. This had a devastating effect on the people living near Mount Fuji, as many of them relied on farming for their food and income.

Another mystery surrounding Fuji's last eruption is the connection between the earthquake that happened shortly before the eruption and the eruption itself. Just 49 days before Mount Fuji erupted, there was a massive earthquake called the Hoei Earthquake. This earthquake was one of the strongest in Japanese history, and it caused widespread damage throughout the region. Some people believe that the earthquake might have triggered the eruption of Mount Fuji by causing the magma inside the volcano to rise toward the surface. However, scientists are still not entirely sure if the earthquake and the eruption were directly related. It's possible that the earthquake weakened the volcanic system, making it easier for the eruption to happen, but it's also possible that the eruption would have occurred even without the earthquake. This is one of the many mysteries that scientists continue to study.

What makes the Hoei Eruption even more puzzling is that it didn't come from the very top of Mount Fuji, where you would normally expect a volcanic eruption to start. Instead, the eruption happened on the side of the mountain, creating a new crater called the Hoei Crater. This crater can still be seen today, and it's one of the most obvious reminders of the eruption. The location of the eruption on the side of the mountain surprised many people because most of Mount Fuji's previous eruptions had come from the summit, or top, of the volcano. The fact that the Hoei Eruption happened in a different place adds another layer of mystery to the event.

Another strange aspect of Mount Fuji's last eruption is how suddenly it started. In some volcanic eruptions, there are warning signs that something is about to happen. For example, there might be small earthquakes or changes in the temperature of the ground near the volcano. But in the case of the Hoei Eruption, there were very few warning signs. People living near Mount Fuji were caught off guard when the eruption began, and they had little time to prepare for the ash and debris that would soon cover their homes and fields. The suddenness of the eruption made it even more dangerous, as many people weren't able to protect themselves or their property in time.

The eruption also had a long-lasting impact on the surrounding environment. The ash that fell from the sky wasn't just a temporary problem—it affected the soil and the water supply for years after the eruption. Farmers had a difficult time growing crops because the ash made the soil less fertile, and some rivers and lakes were contaminated with volcanic debris, making it hard for people to find clean water. In some areas, the ash was so thick that it buried entire villages, and it took a long time for life to return to normal. Even today, scientists can find traces of the ash from the Hoei Eruption in the soil around Mount Fuji, showing just how far-reaching the effects of the eruption were.

One of the most puzzling things about Mount Fuji's last eruption is that it happened during a time of relative peace and stability in Japan. The country was ruled by the Tokugawa shogunate, a powerful military government that had brought an end to years of war and conflict. Under the Tokugawa shoguns, Japan experienced a period of peace known as the Edo period, and the people of Japan were able to focus on farming, trade, and culture. So, when Mount Fuji erupted in 1707, it came as a shock to many people because it disrupted the peaceful life they had become accustomed to. The eruption was a reminder that even during times of peace, nature can still be unpredictable and dangerous.

One of the lingering mysteries about the Hoei Eruption is why Mount Fuji has been so quiet ever since. As we know, Mount Fuji is still considered an active volcano, which means it could erupt again in the future. However, more than 300 years have passed since the Hoei Eruption, and there hasn't been another major eruption since then. This long period of dormancy has led scientists to wonder if Mount Fuji is building up pressure for another eruption or if it's entering a longer period of inactivity. Some scientists believe that the next eruption could be even more powerful than the Hoei Eruption, but no one knows for sure when or if it will happen. This uncertainty adds to the mystery of Mount Fuji's last eruption and keeps people fascinated by the volcano's future.

In addition to the scientific mysteries, there are also many cultural and spiritual beliefs surrounding the Hoei Eruption. In Japanese mythology, Mount Fuji has long been considered a sacred mountain, and some people believed that the eruption was a sign from the gods. They thought that the gods were angry or upset, and the eruption was their way of expressing their displeasure. Even today, some people view Mount Fuji as more than just a natural landmark—they see it as a place of great spiritual significance, and the eruption is often remembered as a powerful and mystical event. The fact that the eruption happened during a time of peace only adds to its legendary status.

The mystery of Fuji's last eruption also includes questions about how future eruptions might affect the modern world. In 1707, Japan was a very different place than it is today. The population was much smaller, and there were no modern technologies like cars, airplanes, or skyscrapers. If Mount Fuji were to erupt again today, the impact would be much greater because Japan is now home to millions of people, and there are many towns and cities built near the base of the mountain. Scientists are constantly studying Mount Fuji to try to predict when the next eruption might happen, but for now, the mountain remains quiet, leaving us to wonder when the mystery of Fuji's eruptions will be solved.

In the end, the mystery of Mount Fuji's last eruption is not just about what happened in 1707—it's about the many questions that remain unanswered today. From the strange way the eruption unfolded to the lasting impact it had on the people and the land, there is still much to learn about this incredible event. And while scientists continue to study Mount Fuji, the mountain itself stands as a reminder of the powerful forces that shape our world, forces that can remain hidden for centuries before suddenly revealing themselves in an explosive and unexpected way.

Chapter 3: Wildlife Around Mount Fuji

The wildlife around Mount Fuji is as fascinating as the mountain itself. This iconic peak, which rises majestically above Japan, isn't just a place of beauty and spirituality for people—it's also home to a wide variety of animals and plants that thrive in the diverse habitats found in the region. Mount Fuji is surrounded by forests, lakes, and open plains, all of which provide homes for many species. The wildlife here has adapted to the unique environment, and some of the animals you might encounter near Mount Fuji can be found nowhere else in Japan. From mammals to birds to insects, Mount Fuji's ecosystem is rich and teeming with life.

One of the most common animals you might see near Mount Fuji is the Japanese macaque, also known as the snow monkey. These monkeys are famous for living in colder regions of Japan, and they're often seen in the forests around the mountain. Snow monkeys are incredibly intelligent and social animals, and they live in groups called troops. They have thick fur that helps keep them warm during the winter months, and they're known for their ability to adapt to a variety of environments. Near Mount Fuji, they can be spotted playing in the trees, foraging for food, or grooming one another, which is an important part of their social behavior. They eat a variety of foods, including fruits, nuts, and insects, and they're always on the lookout for tasty treats.

In addition to snow monkeys, Mount Fuji is also home to a variety of deer species. The most famous of these is the sika deer, which is native to Japan and has been a part of the country's landscape for centuries. Sika deer are known for their beautiful coats, which change with the seasons. In the summer, their fur is reddish-brown with white spots, which helps them blend in with the forest. In the winter, their coats become thicker and turn a darker brown to help them stay warm. Sika deer are graceful and gentle animals, and they can often be seen grazing in the fields and forests around Mount Fuji. They feed on grass, leaves, and twigs, and their presence adds a sense of calm and serenity to the area.

Another interesting animal that lives near Mount Fuji is the Japanese serow. The serow is a type of goat-antelope that is native to Japan, and it looks a bit like a mix between a goat and a deer. It has thick, dark fur and short, curved horns, and it's known for its ability to climb steep, rocky terrain. The serow is a solitary animal, meaning it usually lives alone rather than in groups, and it's most active during the early morning and late afternoon. It feeds on leaves, grasses, and other plants, and it prefers to live in dense forests where it can find plenty of food and shelter. While serows are shy and elusive, lucky hikers might spot one grazing or resting in the shade of the trees near Mount Fuji.

Bird lovers will also find plenty to admire in the wildlife around Mount Fuji. The area is home to a variety of bird species, including some that are unique to Japan. One of the most beautiful birds found here is the Japanese grosbeak, which is known for its striking yellow, black, and white plumage. These birds are often seen perched in the trees, singing their melodious songs or searching for seeds and insects to eat. Another common bird in the area is the Eurasian sparrowhawk, a small bird of prey that hunts other birds and small mammals. With its sharp talons and keen eyesight, the sparrowhawk is a skilled hunter, and it plays an important role in keeping the local ecosystem balanced.

One of the most majestic birds you might see near Mount Fuji is the golden eagle. These powerful birds of prey are known for their incredible hunting skills and their large wingspan, which can reach over seven feet! Golden eagles primarily hunt small mammals like rabbits and hares, but they're also capable of taking down larger prey when necessary. They build their nests in high, remote areas, such as the cliffs and rocky outcrops around Mount Fuji, where they can watch for potential meals from above. Seeing a golden eagle soar through the sky is a breathtaking sight and a reminder of the wild beauty that surrounds Mount Fuji.

Mount Fuji is also home to many smaller creatures, including insects and reptiles. One of the most interesting insects found in the area is the Japanese rhinoceros beetle. These beetles are large, with a distinctive horn on their heads that makes them look a bit like tiny rhinoceroses. They are incredibly strong for their size and are often found in the forests around Mount Fuji, where they feed on tree sap and fruits. Rhinoceros beetles are popular among children in Japan, who sometimes keep them as pets or participate in beetle wrestling competitions. These harmless insects play an important role in the ecosystem by helping to break down decaying plant matter.

Another small but important animal in the region is the Japanese tree frog. These tiny frogs are bright green and have the ability to change color to blend in with their surroundings. They are most active at night, when they hunt for insects to eat, and they can often be heard croaking loudly in the forests around Mount Fuji. Japanese tree frogs are excellent climbers, and they use their sticky toe pads to grip onto leaves, branches, and rocks. Despite their small size, these frogs are an important part of the food chain, providing meals for larger animals like birds and snakes.

Speaking of snakes, there are a few species of reptiles that live near Mount Fuji as well. One of the most common is the Japanese rat snake, a non-venomous snake that helps control the population of small rodents like mice and rats. These snakes are excellent climbers, and they can often be seen slithering through the trees or across the forest floor in search of prey. While they may look a bit intimidating, Japanese rat snakes are harmless to humans and play an important role in maintaining the balance of the local ecosystem.

In addition to the animals, the plant life around Mount Fuji is equally diverse and important. The lower slopes of the mountain are covered in dense forests, which provide food and shelter for many of the animals that live there. One of the most common trees in the area is the Japanese red pine, which grows tall and straight, providing shade and a habitat for birds and insects. Other trees found around Mount Fuji include oak, beech, and cedar, all of which add to the rich biodiversity of the region.

At higher elevations, the vegetation changes as the temperature drops and the air becomes thinner. The forests give way to alpine meadows, where hardy plants like dwarf bamboo and alpine flowers grow. These plants have adapted to the harsh conditions found near the top of the mountain, where the weather can be cold and windy even in the summer. The flowers that bloom in these meadows are often small and delicate, but they add splashes of color to the otherwise rocky landscape.

One of the most iconic plants found near Mount Fuji is the Fujizakura, or Fuji cherry blossom. This tree is native to the area and produces beautiful pink flowers in the spring. The cherry blossoms are a symbol of beauty and renewal in Japanese culture, and the sight of these trees in full bloom against the backdrop of Mount Fuji is truly breathtaking. People come from all over Japan to see the cherry blossoms around Mount Fuji, and they have become an important part of the region's natural beauty.

The lakes around Mount Fuji also provide a unique habitat for wildlife. There are five main lakes in the area, known as the Fuji Five Lakes, and they are home to a variety of fish, amphibians, and birds. One of the most common fish found in the lakes is the Japanese crucian carp, a freshwater fish that thrives in the cool, clear waters. The lakes are also a popular spot for water birds like ducks, herons, and kingfishers, which can be seen fishing or swimming in the calm waters.

The wildlife around Mount Fuji is not only diverse but also important for the health of the ecosystem. Each animal, from the smallest insect to the largest bird of prey, plays a role in keeping the environment balanced. The plants and animals that live in the forests, lakes, and meadows around the mountain have adapted to the unique conditions found here, and they are a vital part of the natural world. Whether you're hiking through the forests, watching birds soar overhead, or listening to the sounds of frogs and insects at night, the wildlife around Mount Fuji is a reminder of the incredible biodiversity that exists in this special part of Japan.

So, while Mount Fuji may be famous for its stunning beauty and spiritual significance, it's also a place of wonder for nature lovers. The animals and plants that call this area home are just as much a part of Mount Fuji's story as the mountain itself, and they help make this region one of the most ecologically rich and fascinating places in Japan. Whether you're a fan of monkeys, birds, insects, or plants, there's something for everyone to discover in the wild world that surrounds Mount Fuji.

Chapter 4: Exploring Fuji's Five Lakes

Exploring Fuji's Five Lakes is like stepping into a world of natural beauty and peaceful serenity. These lakes, known as the Fuji Five Lakes, are located at the northern base of Mount Fuji and offer some of the most breathtaking views of the mountain, as well as opportunities to experience Japan's stunning landscape. Each lake has its own unique charm, and together they create a region that is not only rich in natural beauty but also filled with activities for adventurers and nature lovers. The lakes—Kawaguchi, Yamanaka, Sai, Shoji, and Motosu—are surrounded by lush forests, serene mountains, and picturesque villages, making them a popular destination for visitors from all over the world. Let's take a journey through each of these magnificent lakes and discover what makes them so special.

Lake Kawaguchi, the largest and most popular of the Fuji Five Lakes, is perhaps the most well-known. It is famous for its stunning views of Mount Fuji, which can be seen reflected in the calm waters of the lake on clear days. The view of the mountain from the northern shore of Lake Kawaguchi is one of the most iconic images of Japan. Many visitors come to this lake specifically to photograph Mount Fuji's reflection in the water, a sight that is particularly breathtaking during the cherry blossom season in spring and the vibrant autumn foliage later in the year. The lake is also a hub for outdoor activities such as boating, fishing, and hiking. You can rent rowboats or paddle boats to explore the lake at your own pace, or take a leisurely stroll along the walking paths that surround it. There are also plenty of hot spring resorts in the area, where visitors can relax and soak in the warm, mineral-rich waters while enjoying views of Mount Fuji in the distance.

One of the highlights of Lake Kawaguchi is the Kachi Kachi Ropeway, a cable car that takes visitors up to an observation point on Mount Tenjo. From here, you can enjoy a panoramic view of both Lake Kawaguchi and Mount Fuji. The ride itself is an adventure, offering stunning views as you ascend to the top. At the observation point, you'll find a small shrine dedicated to Mount Fuji and several walking trails that lead to even more viewpoints. The name "Kachi Kachi" comes from a famous Japanese folk tale about a mischievous rabbit and a tanuki (raccoon dog) that is said to have taken place on this very mountain. There's even a statue of the rabbit from the story at the top, making it a fun stop for kids and families.

Lake Yamanaka, the largest lake by surface area in the Fuji Five Lakes region, is known for its cool, refreshing waters and wide-open spaces. This lake is a haven for water sports enthusiasts, as it is one of the few lakes where motorized boats and jet skis are allowed. On any given day, you'll see people sailing, windsurfing, kayaking, and fishing on the lake. The lake is also popular with cyclists, who come to ride around its scenic shoreline. There is a well-maintained cycling path that offers fantastic views of Mount Fuji as you pedal along the water's edge. In the winter, the area around Lake Yamanaka transforms into a winter wonderland, with snow-covered landscapes and opportunities for ice skating and ice fishing. The lake is also home to several campsites, where visitors can set up tents and enjoy a night under the stars with Mount Fuji towering in the background.

One of the most unique experiences at Lake Yamanaka is the swan boats, which are pedal boats shaped like giant swans. These colorful boats can be rented at various spots around the lake, and they're a fun way to explore the water, especially for families with children. As you pedal your swan boat across the lake, you'll have a chance to take in the stunning scenery and enjoy the peaceful atmosphere. Another popular attraction at Lake Yamanaka is Hana no Miyako Park, a large flower park that bursts into bloom during the spring and summer months. The park is filled with fields of colorful flowers, including sunflowers, tulips, and cosmos, and it offers fantastic views of Mount Fuji rising in the distance behind the flowers. It's a perfect spot for a picnic or a leisurely walk among the blossoms.

Lake Sai, the third-largest of the Fuji Five Lakes, is known for its peaceful, untouched beauty. Unlike the more developed lakes like Kawaguchi and Yamanaka, Lake Sai has remained relatively quiet and undeveloped, making it an ideal destination for those looking to escape the crowds and enjoy nature in its purest form. The lake is surrounded by dense forests and rolling hills, and it's a great place for hiking, birdwatching, and fishing. There are several hiking trails that start from the shores of Lake Sai and lead into the surrounding mountains, offering stunning views of both the lake and Mount Fuji. One of the most popular trails is the Aokigahara Forest Trail, which takes you through the mysterious and dense Aokigahara Forest, also known as the "Sea of Trees." This forest is famous for its twisted trees and lava caves, and it has a reputation for being haunted, adding an air of mystery to your hike.

For those who enjoy camping, Lake Sai is a fantastic spot to set up a tent and spend a night under the stars. There are several campsites around the lake, many of which offer beautiful views of Mount Fuji and easy access to the hiking trails. The lake itself is perfect for canoeing or kayaking, and the calm waters make it a peaceful place to paddle. If you're looking for a unique experience, you can visit the nearby Iyashi no Sato, a reconstructed traditional village where you can learn about Japan's rural past. The village features traditional thatched-roof houses, many of which have been turned into museums, craft shops, and cafes. It's a great place to experience Japan's history and culture while enjoying the natural beauty of Lake Sai.

Lake Shoji, the smallest of the Fuji Five Lakes, is often called the "Hidden Lake" because it is tucked away between the larger lakes of Sai and Motosu. Despite its small size, Lake Shoji offers some of the most stunning views of Mount Fuji, especially in the early morning when the lake is calm and the reflection of the mountain is perfectly mirrored in the water. Lake Shoji is a popular destination for photographers, who come to capture the beauty of Mount Fuji at sunrise and sunset.

The lake is also known for its excellent fishing, with anglers coming to catch trout, bass, and other freshwater fish. Like Lake Sai, Lake Shoji is relatively undeveloped, and it's a peaceful place to relax and enjoy the natural surroundings.

Because of its small size, Lake Shoji feels more intimate and secluded than some of the other lakes, and it's a great spot for a quiet picnic or a leisurely paddle in a rowboat. The surrounding area is filled with hiking trails that lead through forests and up into the hills, where you can enjoy panoramic views of the lake and Mount Fuji. If you're lucky, you might even spot some of the local wildlife, such as deer, birds, and small mammals, as you explore the area. Lake Shoji is also close to several hot spring resorts, where you can soak in natural hot springs while taking in views of the lake and the mountain.

Lake Motosu, the deepest and clearest of the Fuji Five Lakes, is famous for being featured on the back of the Japanese 1,000 yen note. The view of Mount Fuji from the northern shore of Lake Motosu, with the mountain reflected in the clear blue waters, is one of the most iconic images of Japan. This lake is a favorite among swimmers and divers, as the water is incredibly clear and clean. In fact, Lake Motosu is so clear that you can often see down to the bottom, even in the deepest parts. The lake is surrounded by rugged mountains and dense forests, making it a perfect spot for hiking and exploring the natural beauty of the region.

One of the most popular activities at Lake Motosu is camping. There are several campsites along the shore, many of which offer stunning views of Mount Fuji. Camping at Lake Motosu is a great way to experience the beauty of the area up close, and it's especially magical at night when the stars come out and the reflection of the mountain can be seen in the calm waters. For those who enjoy water sports, Lake Motosu is a great place for kayaking, stand-up paddleboarding, and even windsurfing, thanks to the steady winds that blow across the lake.

In addition to its natural beauty, the Fuji Five Lakes region is steeped in history and culture. The area has long been considered a sacred place, with Mount Fuji being a symbol of beauty, power, and spirituality in Japan. Over the centuries, many pilgrims have traveled to the Fuji Five Lakes region to pay their respects to the mountain, and today, the lakes continue to attract visitors from all over the world who come to enjoy the stunning scenery and experience the magic of Mount Fuji up close. Whether you're hiking through the forests, paddling across the lakes, or simply sitting by the shore and taking in the view, the Fuji Five Lakes offer a unique and unforgettable experience.

In conclusion, exploring Fuji's Five Lakes is a journey into the heart of Japan's natural beauty. Each lake has its own character and charm, and together they create a region that is rich in both scenery and adventure. Whether you're looking for outdoor activities, peaceful relaxation, or simply a place to admire Mount Fuji's majestic presence, the Fuji Five Lakes are the perfect destination.

Chapter 5: The Samurai Legends of Mount Fuji

The Samurai legends of Mount Fuji are stories full of bravery, honor, and deep connection with Japan's most iconic mountain. These tales have been passed down through generations, and they help keep the spirit of Japan's famous warriors alive in the shadow of Mount Fuji. The samurai were the noble warriors of ancient Japan, known for their skills in combat, their strict code of honor called bushido, and their loyalty to their lords. Mount Fuji, as Japan's tallest and most sacred mountain, has long been a symbol of strength and resilience, qualities that the samurai admired. Over the centuries, many legends about the samurai and their relationship with Mount Fuji have grown, blending the natural power of the mountain with the human strength of these brave warriors.

One of the most famous samurai legends tied to Mount Fuji is the story of Minamoto no Yoritomo. Yoritomo was the founder of the Kamakura shogunate, one of Japan's most powerful military governments. In the late 12th century, Yoritomo rose to power after many years of conflict and war. As a young man, he had been exiled by a rival clan and forced to live in hiding, but he never gave up his dream of restoring his family's honor and taking control of Japan. According to legend, during his time in exile, Yoritomo often gazed at Mount Fuji from a distance and drew strength from its towering presence. The mountain became a symbol of his determination to overcome obstacles and reclaim his rightful place as a leader. In the end, Yoritomo succeeded, and he established a new era of samurai rule in Japan. The connection between Yoritomo's rise to power and the strength of Mount Fuji became part of the samurai mythology, showing how the mountain's majestic presence could inspire warriors to achieve greatness.

Another samurai legend connected to Mount Fuji is the tale of Nitta Yoshisada. Nitta Yoshisada was a samurai warrior who lived in the 14th century during a time of civil war in Japan. He was a loyal supporter of Emperor Go-Daigo, who was trying to regain control of the country from the powerful shogun. Yoshisada led his army in several battles against the shogun's forces, and he became famous for his courage and loyalty to the emperor. One of the most dramatic moments in Yoshisada's story takes place near Mount Fuji. During a critical battle, Yoshisada's army was cornered by the enemy and had no way to escape. According to the legend, Yoshisada prayed to Mount Fuji for guidance and strength. He believed that the mountain's sacred power would protect him and his men. Inspired by the mountain's strength, Yoshisada and his warriors fought bravely and managed to break through the enemy lines. Though Yoshisada's ultimate fate was tragic—he eventually died in battle—his story became a symbol of the samurai's unwavering loyalty and bravery, with Mount Fuji standing as a silent witness to his final moments of glory.

In addition to individual stories of famous samurai, there are also legends about entire groups of warriors who found inspiration and refuge around Mount Fuji. One such legend is the story of the Takeda clan, a powerful family of samurai who ruled over a large part of central Japan during the 16th century. The Takeda clan was known for their fierce warriors and their loyalty to their leader, Takeda Shingen. Shingen was a brilliant military strategist and one of the most feared samurai generals of his time. He often used Mount Fuji as a symbol of his clan's power, comparing the strength and resilience of his warriors to the unshakable presence of the mountain. According to legend, Shingen would lead his men in rituals of prayer and meditation near Mount Fuji before going into battle, seeking the mountain's blessing and protection. The Takeda clan believed that by honoring Mount Fuji, they could draw on its power to ensure their victory in battle. Although the Takeda clan eventually fell, their connection to Mount Fuji became part of the samurai lore, representing the deep respect that the warriors had for the natural world and its ability to influence their fate.

Mount Fuji also plays a significant role in the legend of the 47 Ronin, one of the most famous stories of samurai loyalty and revenge. This story takes place in the early 18th century, during the Edo period, when Japan was at peace under the rule of the Tokugawa shogunate. The 47 Ronin were samurai who had lost their master, Lord Asano, after he was forced to commit seppuku, or ritual suicide, for attacking a corrupt official named Kira. Without a master, the samurai became ronin, or masterless warriors. Despite their situation, the 47 Ronin remained loyal to their fallen lord and secretly plotted to avenge his death. After months of careful planning, they stormed Kira's mansion and killed him, restoring their honor. In one version of the legend, the ronin stopped at Mount Fuji during their journey to Kira's mansion, where they prayed for strength and guidance. The mountain's towering presence reminded them of their duty and their commitment to justice, and it gave them the courage to carry out their mission. After their successful revenge, the 47 Ronin became symbols of the samurai code of honor, and their connection to Mount Fuji added to the mystique of their story.

The samurai legends of Mount Fuji aren't just limited to historical figures and battles—they also include tales of supernatural encounters. In many of these stories, the mountain is seen as a mystical place where samurai warriors would go to seek wisdom, strength, or even immortality. One such legend tells of a group of samurai who climbed Mount Fuji in search of a legendary elixir of life that was said to be hidden at the mountain's peak. The elixir was believed to grant eternal life to anyone who drank it, and the samurai were determined to find it. After a long and difficult journey, they finally reached the summit, but instead of finding the elixir, they encountered a powerful spirit who guarded the mountain. The spirit warned the samurai that true immortality could only be found through living a life of honor and virtue, not by seeking shortcuts to eternal life. The samurai, realizing the wisdom in the spirit's words, returned to their homes with a renewed sense of purpose, determined to live their lives according to the samurai code of bushido.

Another supernatural legend involves the tengu, mythical creatures often depicted as part human and part bird, who were believed to live in the mountains and forests of Japan. The tengu were known as fierce warriors and were said to have taught swordsmanship to the most skilled samurai. According to legend, some samurai would climb Mount Fuji to train with the tengu, hoping to learn their powerful fighting techniques. The tengu were said to be strict teachers, testing the samurai's strength, courage, and dedication before passing on their secret knowledge. Only the most disciplined and honorable warriors could earn the tengu's favor and learn their skills. This legend highlights the samurai's respect for the natural world and their belief in the importance of discipline and hard work in achieving greatness.

In yet another legend, Mount Fuji is said to be the home of an ancient dragon that protects the land and its people. Samurai warriors, recognizing the dragon's power, would sometimes journey to the mountain to offer prayers and seek the dragon's protection before going into battle. The dragon was believed to grant its blessing to those who were pure of heart and strong in spirit, ensuring their victory in battle. For the samurai, the dragon of Mount Fuji became a symbol of both the danger and the majesty of the mountain, and its presence in the legends added to the sense of mystery and power surrounding the samurai's connection to Fuji.

The samurai legends of Mount Fuji reflect the deep respect that Japan's warriors had for their natural surroundings. The mountain, with its towering height and perfect shape, symbolized the strength, endurance, and honor that the samurai strived to embody. For many samurai, Mount Fuji was more than just a mountain—it was a source of inspiration, a place of spiritual significance, and a symbol of the ideals they held most dear. Whether seeking strength before a battle, praying for guidance during difficult times, or searching for wisdom in the mountain's heights, the samurai's connection to Mount Fuji is a powerful reminder of the importance of nature in Japanese culture and the timeless appeal of these legendary warriors.

Chapter 6: Climbing Mount Fuji: A Tradition

Climbing Mount Fuji has been a long-standing tradition that draws people from all over the world, but especially the people of Japan. For centuries, scaling the slopes of this magnificent mountain has been more than just an adventurous hike; it is a deeply spiritual journey, a test of endurance, and a cultural experience that connects modern climbers to generations of those who have made the pilgrimage before them. Standing tall at 3,776 meters (12,389 feet), Mount Fuji is Japan's highest peak, and its perfectly symmetrical shape makes it one of the most recognizable mountains in the world. The tradition of climbing Fuji, or "Fujisan," as it is known in Japan, goes back hundreds of years, deeply rooted in religious practices and spiritual beliefs, and today, it remains a popular activity for adventurers, tourists, and those seeking to connect with Japan's cultural heritage.

The origins of climbing Mount Fuji are closely tied to Japan's religious history. For many centuries, Mount Fuji has been considered a sacred site in both the Shinto and Buddhist faiths. In Shinto, the native religion of Japan, Fuji is believed to be the home of a powerful goddess, Konohanasakuya-hime, the goddess of Mount Fuji and all volcanoes. She is associated with life, growth, and the delicate beauty of cherry blossoms, but she is also a symbol of the unpredictable power of nature. In Buddhist traditions, Mount Fuji is often seen as a gateway to enlightenment, with its peak representing a place closer to the heavens. As a result, climbing the mountain was initially a religious practice, with monks and pilgrims making the long and arduous trek to the summit as a form of worship and meditation. For these early climbers, reaching the top of Mount Fuji was not just about conquering the physical challenge, but about purifying the soul and achieving spiritual fulfillment.

One of the oldest known climbers of Mount Fuji was a Buddhist monk named En no Gyoja, who is said to have reached the summit in the 7th century. En no Gyoja was a mystic and ascetic who practiced a form of mountain worship known as Shugendo, which combined elements of Shinto, Buddhism, and Taoism. For him and his followers, climbing sacred mountains like Fuji was a way to connect with the divine and gain spiritual powers. Over the centuries, more and more pilgrims began to follow in his footsteps, and the tradition of climbing Fuji as a spiritual journey continued to grow. By the Edo period (1603-1868), organized groups of pilgrims known as Fuji-ko were making regular trips to the mountain, and climbing Mount Fuji became an important ritual in Japanese religious life.

During the Edo period, Fuji-ko groups were formed in towns and villages all over Japan, and their sole purpose was to organize pilgrimages to Mount Fuji. These groups were often led by local priests or elders, and they would prepare for months before making the journey. The pilgrimage to Mount Fuji was not an easy one. Before modern transportation, pilgrims would have to walk for days, sometimes weeks, just to reach the base of the mountain. Once they arrived, they would purify themselves in sacred springs and offer prayers at the shrines located at the foot of the mountain. Then, they would begin the long climb to the summit, often stopping at various stations along the way to rest and perform more rituals. The climb itself was seen as a form of ascetic practice, with the physical hardship of the journey helping to cleanse the body and mind. Reaching the summit at sunrise, known as "Goraiko," was the ultimate goal, as it was believed to bring spiritual enlightenment and blessings for the climbers and their families.

As the tradition of climbing Mount Fuji grew, so did the infrastructure to support the pilgrims. Along the various trails leading up the mountain, small huts were built to provide shelter for climbers, and shrines were established at key points where prayers could be offered. The most famous of these shrines is the Fujisan Hongu Sengen Taisha Shrine, located at the foot of the mountain in the city of Fujinomiya. This shrine, which dates back over 1,000 years, is dedicated to Konohanasakuya-hime, and it has long been a starting point for pilgrims making the climb. Even today, many climbers stop at the shrine to pray for a safe journey before beginning their ascent. There are also several other smaller shrines and temples scattered around the base of the mountain, each with its own unique connection to the history and spirituality of Mount Fuji.

Although the tradition of climbing Mount Fuji has its roots in religion, over time it became more of a cultural and recreational activity. In the late 19th century, after Japan opened its doors to the West during the Meiji Restoration, foreigners began to take an interest in climbing Mount Fuji. One of the most famous early Western climbers was Sir Rutherford Alcock, a British diplomat, who successfully reached the summit in 1860, becoming the first recorded non-Japanese person to do so. Alcock's climb helped to popularize Mount Fuji among foreigners, and soon, the mountain was attracting adventurers and explorers from all over the world.

Today, climbing Mount Fuji has become a rite of passage for many Japanese people and visitors alike. Every summer, during the official climbing season from July to September, thousands of people make the journey to the top. The trails that were once used by pilgrims are now well-marked paths, and the mountain is dotted with huts where climbers can rest, eat, and sleep during their ascent. There are four main trails leading to the summit, each offering a different experience. The Yoshida Trail is the most popular and well-traveled, while the Fujinomiya, Subashiri, and Gotemba trails provide more of a challenge for those looking for a less crowded climb. Despite the modern conveniences, the climb is still a physically demanding experience. It typically takes between five to ten hours to reach the summit, depending on the trail and the climber's pace, and the altitude makes the air thinner, which can cause altitude sickness. However, the sense of accomplishment that comes with standing at the top of Japan's highest mountain is something that keeps climbers coming back year after year.

One of the most memorable parts of the climb is watching the sunrise from the summit. This experience, known as "Goraiko," is considered one of the most beautiful and spiritual moments of the journey. Climbers often time their ascent so that they reach the top just as the sun begins to rise over the horizon. The sight of the first rays of sunlight illuminating the clouds and the surrounding landscape is breathtaking, and for many, it is a deeply emotional and spiritual experience. Some climbers even say that watching the sunrise from Mount Fuji feels like a rebirth, as if the hardships of the climb have purified them, and the new day represents a fresh start.

In addition to the spiritual and cultural aspects of climbing Mount Fuji, there is also a strong sense of community among climbers. Because the climb is so popular, especially during the peak season, it is common to find yourself surrounded by hundreds of other climbers, all making the journey together. This creates a unique atmosphere of camaraderie and shared experience. Strangers become friends as they help each other along the way, sharing snacks, water, and words of encouragement. For many, the sense of connection with fellow climbers is one of the highlights of the journey.

Although climbing Mount Fuji is primarily a summer activity, some experienced mountaineers choose to climb during the off-season, when the mountain is covered in snow. This is a much more dangerous and challenging endeavor, requiring special equipment and training. However, for those who are up to the challenge, winter climbing offers a completely different experience of Mount Fuji's beauty, with snow-covered slopes and a much quieter, more peaceful atmosphere.

Climbing Mount Fuji is not just about reaching the summit. It is about the journey itself, the connection to nature, the bond with fellow climbers, and the sense of accomplishment that comes with conquering

Japan's most famous mountain. For many people, it is a deeply personal experience, a chance to challenge themselves both physically and mentally, and to reflect on their own life's journey. Whether climbing as part of a long-standing tradition, seeking spiritual enlightenment, or simply looking for an unforgettable adventure, the experience of climbing Mount Fuji is one that leaves a lasting impression on everyone who makes the journey.

Chapter 7: The Ancient Shrines of Fuji

The ancient shrines of Mount Fuji hold deep significance in Japanese culture and religion, as they represent a connection between the natural world and the spiritual realm. For centuries, people have worshipped the mountain, viewing it as a sacred place that holds great power and mystery. The shrines scattered around the base and slopes of Mount Fuji are not just places of prayer, but symbols of reverence for the mountain itself. These shrines, some of which are thousands of years old, are dedicated to various deities, particularly the mountain goddess Konohanasakuya-hime, who is believed to be the protector of Fuji and all volcanoes in Japan. Visiting these shrines is not just a religious act, but a way for people to show respect to the forces of nature and the ancient traditions that have been passed down through generations.

One of the most important and oldest shrines associated with Mount Fuji is the Fujisan Hongu Sengen Taisha Shrine. This shrine, located at the foot of the mountain in the town of Fujinomiya, dates back over 1,000 years and is considered the head shrine of more than 1,300 Sengen shrines found throughout Japan. The shrine is dedicated to Konohanasakuya-hime, who is often depicted as a beautiful woman surrounded by cherry blossoms. According to legend, she is the goddess who resides on Mount Fuji, and she is believed to control the eruptions of the volcano. People pray to her for protection against natural disasters, particularly volcanic eruptions, as well as for safe childbirth and a prosperous life. The shrine's location at the base of Mount Fuji is significant because it is the starting point for pilgrims and climbers who wish to make the journey to the summit. Before beginning their climb, they stop at the shrine to purify themselves in the sacred waters of the Wakutama Pond, a spring that is said to be fed by the melted snow from Mount Fuji itself. The shrine's grand torii gate and towering trees create a peaceful and solemn atmosphere, making it a place of quiet reflection for visitors.

Another ancient shrine connected to Mount Fuji is the Kitaguchi Hongu Fuji Sengen Shrine, located on the northern side of the mountain in the town of Fujiyoshida. Like Fujisan Hongu Sengen Taisha, this shrine is also dedicated to Konohanasakuya-hime and has been a place of worship for pilgrims for centuries. The shrine's history dates back to the 7th century, when it was built to honor the mountain goddess and protect the surrounding villages from volcanic eruptions. Kitaguchi Hongu Fuji Sengen Shrine served as the starting point for pilgrims who followed the Yoshida Trail, one of the main routes used to climb Mount Fuji. In the past, pilgrims would gather at the shrine to pray for a safe journey before beginning their ascent. The shrine grounds are home to several ancient cedar trees, some of which are believed to be over 1,000 years old. These towering trees add to the mystical atmosphere of the shrine, making it feel like a place where the natural and spiritual worlds come together. The main hall of the shrine is an impressive structure with a thatched roof and intricate wood carvings, and it stands as a reminder of the long history of devotion to Mount Fuji.

In addition to the larger, more well-known shrines, there are many smaller, lesser-known shrines scattered around the mountain's base and along its trails. These shrines are often located in remote, hard-to-reach areas, but they are important to the locals who continue to honor the traditions of Mount Fuji worship. For example, the Komitake Shrine, located on the lower slopes of Mount Fuji, is believed to be the site where ancient mountain worshippers, known as Shugendo practitioners, would perform rituals to honor the spirits of the mountain. Shugendo is a Japanese folk religion that blends elements of Buddhism, Shinto, and Taoism, and its practitioners believe that mountains are sacred places where humans can connect with the divine. The Komitake Shrine is one of the oldest shrines on Mount Fuji, and it holds special significance for those who follow the Shugendo tradition. The shrine is also said to mark the site of an ancient volcanic eruption, and its presence serves as a reminder of the mountain's powerful and sometimes destructive nature.

Another fascinating shrine connected to Mount Fuji is the Okumiya Shrine, which is located at the summit of the mountain. This shrine is the highest Shinto shrine in all of Japan, and it is the final destination for many climbers who make the long journey to the top of Mount Fuji. The Okumiya Shrine is dedicated to Konohanasakuya-hime, and reaching it is considered a deeply spiritual achievement for many climbers. In the past, only monks and priests were allowed to visit the summit, as it was believed to be too sacred for ordinary people. However, as time went on, more and more people were permitted to make the pilgrimage to the top. Today, anyone who reaches the summit of Mount Fuji can visit the Okumiya Shrine, where they can offer prayers and reflect on the journey they've just completed. The small, simple structure of the shrine contrasts with the vastness of the surrounding landscape, and many climbers describe a feeling of awe and reverence as they stand at the top of Japan's most iconic mountain, looking out over the clouds and the distant horizon.

The ancient shrines of Mount Fuji are not just places of worship; they are living symbols of Japan's cultural and religious heritage. Each shrine has its own unique history, but they are all connected by the deep respect that people have for the mountain. Over the centuries, these shrines have played an important role in preserving the traditions of Mount Fuji worship, and they continue to be places where people can find spiritual solace and a connection to nature. Even today, thousands of people visit the shrines around Mount Fuji each year, whether to pray for good fortune, to seek protection from natural disasters, or simply to pay their respects to the mountain that has stood as a symbol of Japan for millennia.

For many, visiting these shrines is an integral part of the experience of climbing Mount Fuji. Before setting off on the journey to the summit, climbers often stop at one of the shrines to offer prayers and ask for blessings. This act of devotion helps to connect modern-day climbers with the long history of pilgrims who have made the same journey for hundreds of years. The shrines serve as reminders that Mount Fuji is not just a physical challenge to be conquered, but a sacred place that has been revered for centuries.

As Japan has modernized, the role of these ancient shrines has evolved, but their significance has not diminished. Today, they continue to be important cultural landmarks, attracting not only pilgrims and worshippers but also tourists and history enthusiasts who want to learn more about the spiritual traditions of Mount Fuji. The shrines also play a vital role in preserving the natural environment around the mountain. Many of the shrines are located in protected areas, and the priests who oversee them work to ensure that the natural beauty of Mount Fuji is preserved for future generations.

In addition to their religious significance, the shrines of Mount Fuji also serve as important cultural and historical sites. They are places where traditional Japanese architecture, art, and craftsmanship can be seen and appreciated. The intricate wood carvings, colorful torii gates, and serene gardens that surround the shrines are all examples of the deep connection between Japan's spiritual beliefs and its artistic traditions. For those who visit these shrines, they offer not only a place of prayer and reflection but also a glimpse into Japan's rich cultural history.

Overall, the ancient shrines of Mount Fuji are much more than just religious sites. They are symbols of the deep respect and reverence that the people of Japan have for their natural environment and for the spiritual forces that they believe reside in the world around them. The shrines remind us that Mount Fuji is not just a mountain, but a sacred place that has been worshipped and admired for centuries. Through these shrines, the legacy of Mount Fuji worship continues to thrive, and they remain an integral part of Japan's cultural and spiritual identity.

Chapter 8: Fuji in Japanese Art and Culture

Mount Fuji, with its striking, symmetrical shape and towering presence, has been a source of inspiration for Japanese artists and a symbol of Japan's culture for centuries. It's not just a mountain; it's an iconic figure that has come to represent beauty, power, and even the spiritual essence of the country. The snow-capped peak of Mount Fuji can be seen from hundreds of kilometers away, and its impressive size makes it a natural focus for creative minds. Over time, Fuji has appeared in countless works of art, literature, poetry, and even modern media, making it one of the most famous mountains in the world. From ancient times to the present, its image has been lovingly captured by artists of every generation, helping shape the cultural identity of Japan.

One of the most famous artists to depict Mount Fuji was Katsushika Hokusai, a legendary ukiyo-e artist from the Edo period (1603–1868). Hokusai's series "Thirty-Six Views of Mount Fuji" is perhaps the most well-known artistic representation of the mountain. This series of woodblock prints, created in the early 1830s, showcases Fuji from various perspectives and in different seasons. In each print, the mountain takes on new forms—sometimes looming large in the background, other times peeking out subtly behind everyday scenes of village life. Hokusai's use of vibrant colors, delicate lines, and creative compositions turned Mount Fuji into a global icon. The most famous print in this series is undoubtedly "The Great Wave off Kanagawa," in which a gigantic wave threatens to engulf boats while Mount Fuji sits calmly in the background, a symbol of stability amidst chaos. This single image has become a symbol of both the power of nature and the resilience of the human spirit, and it's one of the most recognized works of Japanese art in the world.

Hokusai wasn't the only artist to be captivated by Mount Fuji. Another great ukiyo-e artist, Utagawa Hiroshige, also created a series of prints featuring the mountain. Hiroshige's "Fifty-Three Stations of the Tōkaidō" series depicts various locations along the famous Tōkaidō road, which connected Edo (now Tokyo) to Kyoto. Many of these prints feature Mount Fuji in the distance, reminding travelers that the mountain was a constant companion on their journey. While Hokusai focused on bold, dramatic compositions, Hiroshige's prints are known for their serene, atmospheric beauty. His depictions of Fuji often show the mountain shrouded in mist or reflected in the calm waters of lakes, creating a sense of peaceful harmony with nature.

Beyond the world of ukiyo-e, Mount Fuji has also played a significant role in Japanese literature. Poets from ancient times to modern days have written about the mountain, often using it as a metaphor for strength, endurance, or transcendence. In classical Japanese poetry, known as waka, Fuji was frequently praised for its majestic beauty. One famous example comes from the 8th-century anthology "Man'yōshū," which contains several poems dedicated to Mount Fuji. These poems reflect the deep respect and admiration that the people of Japan felt for the mountain, viewing it as a divine presence. As the tallest mountain in Japan, Fuji was believed to be the dwelling place of gods, and its ever-present snowcap added to its mystical allure. Poets would often compare the mountain to a god or a great leader, symbolizing unshakable power and grace.

In the centuries that followed, Mount Fuji continued to be a favorite subject for writers and poets. During the Heian period (794–1185), Fuji was often mentioned in court poetry, where it was celebrated not only for its physical beauty but also for its spiritual significance. Many poets saw Fuji as a symbol of immortality, as its peak seemed to reach toward the heavens, making it a bridge between the earthly and the divine. In later periods, during the Edo and Meiji eras, Fuji became a popular subject in haiku poetry, where its simple yet awe-inspiring form could be captured in just a few lines. Even today, poets and writers draw on Fuji's powerful symbolism to express themes of perseverance, natural beauty, and the eternal flow of time.

In addition to its influence on visual art and literature, Mount Fuji has played a central role in Japanese religion and spirituality. For centuries, the mountain has been considered sacred, particularly in the Shinto and Buddhist traditions. In Shinto, the indigenous religion of Japan, Fuji is believed to be the home of Konohanasakuya-hime, the goddess of Mount Fuji and all volcanoes. Pilgrims have climbed the mountain for centuries as a form of spiritual purification, seeking to connect with the divine by ascending closer to the heavens. During the Edo period, a religious group known as the Fuji-ko became popular. Members of this group worshipped Mount Fuji and would regularly make pilgrimages to its summit. Climbing Fuji was seen as a way to achieve enlightenment and gain protection from misfortune, and many pilgrims would leave offerings at the shrines located at the mountain's base and on its slopes.

Buddhism also views Mount Fuji as a place of great spiritual power. Some Buddhist sects see the mountain as a symbol of the Buddha's teachings, representing the journey toward enlightenment. In Buddhist imagery, the mountain's peak can symbolize the ultimate goal of attaining Nirvana, while the slopes represent the various challenges and obstacles one must overcome on the spiritual path. Throughout history, monks and ascetics have retreated to the mountain's caves and forests to meditate and seek enlightenment, drawn by the serene and isolated environment.

Mount Fuji's cultural significance extends beyond traditional art and religion. In modern times, it has appeared in everything from films to video games, cementing its place as a symbol of Japanese identity in the global imagination. Its image is often used to promote tourism, appearing on postcards, posters, and souvenirs, and it has become a must-see destination for travelers from around the world. The mountain's near-perfect cone shape, often capped with snow, is instantly recognizable, making it a symbol not just of Japan's natural beauty, but also of its cultural heritage. Its role as a symbol of national pride was further solidified when it was named a UNESCO World Heritage site in 2013, recognized for both its natural and cultural significance.

Fuji has even made its way into modern popular culture, appearing in countless movies, television shows, and manga. It's often used as a backdrop in stories that emphasize the beauty of Japan's landscapes or the endurance of its people. For example, in anime and manga, Mount Fuji is frequently shown in scenes of quiet reflection or during moments of personal growth for characters. The mountain serves as a reminder of nature's grandeur and the importance of harmony with the environment. In many ways, Fuji's presence in modern media continues the tradition of reverence and admiration that has surrounded the mountain for centuries.

The cultural importance of Mount Fuji is also evident in Japanese festivals and celebrations. Every year, festivals are held in honor of the mountain, particularly in the towns and cities that surround it. One such festival is the Fujisan Hongu Sengen Taisha Shrine Festival, which takes place in the town of Fujinomiya. During this festival, locals gather to celebrate the mountain and pray for protection from eruptions and other natural disasters. The festival includes traditional music, dance performances, and rituals that date back hundreds of years, all of which are meant to honor the mountain and its guardian goddess, Konohanasakuya-hime.

In addition to religious festivals, Mount Fuji is also the focus of many art and music festivals, where artists, musicians, and performers gather to celebrate the mountain's cultural influence. These festivals often feature exhibitions of artwork inspired by Fuji, as well as concerts and performances that take place in view of the mountain. These events help to keep the cultural significance of Mount Fuji alive, reminding both locals and visitors of the mountain's enduring importance in Japanese society.

As Japan has modernized, Mount Fuji's role in the country's culture has evolved, but its significance has never diminished. While it was once primarily a religious symbol, today it represents a broader sense of national identity and pride. Whether through traditional art, literature, or modern media, Mount Fuji continues to inspire and captivate people around the world. Its image has come to symbolize not just the beauty of Japan, but also its rich cultural history, its connection to nature, and the resilience of its people. Even in a rapidly changing world, Mount Fuji remains a constant, reminding us of the timeless beauty and power of nature and the lasting influence of Japan's cultural heritage.

Chapter 9: The Sacred Festivals of Mount Fuji

Mount Fuji, with its towering height and graceful slopes, is not only one of Japan's most iconic natural landmarks but also a deeply spiritual place. Over the centuries, it has been the center of many sacred festivals and rituals, reflecting its profound significance in Japanese religion and culture. These festivals are not just local events; they are deeply rooted in Japan's history, bringing together people from all over the country and beyond to honor the mountain, seek blessings, and connect with ancient traditions.

One of the most important and well-known festivals associated with Mount Fuji is the Fujisan Hongu Sengen Taisha Festival, which takes place at the Fujisan Hongu Sengen Taisha Shrine in the town of Fujinomiya, located at the base of Mount Fuji. This shrine is considered one of the most important Shinto shrines dedicated to the goddess Konohanasakuya-hime, the deity who is believed to protect Mount Fuji and control the volcano's eruptions. The festival, which takes place every year in May, is a vibrant and colorful event that lasts for several days. It includes a variety of traditional rituals, performances, and processions, all of which are meant to honor the goddess and seek her blessings for the safety of the people living near the mountain.

The Fujisan Hongu Sengen Taisha Festival is a major event in the region, attracting thousands of visitors and pilgrims. One of the highlights of the festival is the Yabusame archery performance, where skilled horseback archers dressed in traditional samurai armor gallop along a track while shooting arrows at wooden targets. This ancient form of archery dates back to Japan's medieval period and is performed as a way of offering prayers to the gods for protection and good fortune. The sight of the archers riding at full speed while maintaining perfect accuracy is both thrilling and awe-inspiring, and it connects the audience with Japan's rich cultural past.

Another key part of the Fujisan Hongu Sengen Taisha Festival is the procession of portable shrines, known as mikoshi. These elaborately decorated shrines, which are carried on the shoulders of participants, are believed to house the spirits of the gods. As the mikoshi are paraded through the streets, people cheer, clap, and chant, creating an atmosphere of joy and celebration. The procession eventually makes its way toward the shrine, where the mikoshi are placed in front of the main sanctuary as offerings to Konohanasakuya-hime. The act of carrying the mikoshi is seen as a way of inviting the gods to join the festival, and it symbolizes the deep connection between the people and the divine.

In addition to the main festival in May, there are several other smaller festivals and rituals that take place throughout the year at the various shrines around Mount Fuji. One of these is the Fuji Fire Festival, or Yoshida Fire Festival, which takes place in late August in the town of Fujiyoshida. This festival is held to mark the end of the official climbing season for Mount Fuji, which runs from July to September. The festival is a dramatic and fiery celebration, with huge torches and bonfires lit throughout the town. The purpose of the festival is to calm the spirit of Mount Fuji and prevent future eruptions, as well as to give thanks for a successful climbing season.

The Fuji Fire Festival has a long history, dating back over 500 years. It begins with a procession of people carrying portable shrines through the streets of Fujiyoshida, followed by the lighting of large torches known as taimatsu. These torches, some of which are several meters tall, are placed along the main streets and set ablaze as night falls, creating a spectacular sight. The flames from the torches are said to purify the area and protect the town from natural disasters. The festival lasts for two days, and during this time, the streets are filled with the sound of traditional music and the lively atmosphere of festival-goers celebrating the end of the climbing season.

One of the most important religious rituals associated with Mount Fuji is the Oharai, or purification ceremony, which takes place at many of the shrines around the mountain. The Oharai is a Shinto ritual that is performed to cleanse people of impurities and ensure their spiritual well-being. At the Fujisan Hongu Sengen Taisha Shrine, this ritual is often performed for pilgrims who have come to climb Mount Fuji. Before beginning their ascent, the pilgrims receive a blessing from the shrine's priests, who use sacred branches and chant prayers to purify the climbers and ensure their safe journey up the mountain. The Oharai ceremony is an essential part of the spiritual experience of climbing Mount Fuji, as it connects the climbers with the gods and helps them prepare for the physical and mental challenges ahead.

For centuries, Mount Fuji has also been the center of various religious pilgrimages, particularly for followers of the Fuji-ko religion. The Fuji-ko is a religious sect that emerged during the Edo period (1603–1868) and is dedicated to the worship of Mount Fuji as a sacred entity. The followers of Fuji-ko believe that climbing Mount Fuji is a form of spiritual purification, and they would often make pilgrimages to the mountain's summit as part of their religious practice. Even today, many people who climb Mount Fuji see it as more than just a physical challenge; it is a deeply spiritual journey that allows them to connect with the gods and the natural world.

During the summer months, when the weather is suitable for climbing, Mount Fuji becomes a bustling hub of activity as pilgrims, tourists, and climbers from all over the world come to ascend its slopes. Many of these climbers participate in rituals and prayers before starting their ascent, and they often stop at the mountain's various shrines and sacred sites along the way. One of the most important of these is the Okumiya Shrine, located at the summit of Mount Fuji. This shrine, which is dedicated to Konohanasakuya-hime, is the highest shrine in

Japan, and reaching it is seen as the ultimate achievement for many pilgrims. Upon reaching the summit, climbers often make offerings and prayers, asking for blessings and giving thanks for their successful journey.

Another unique festival associated with Mount Fuji is the Shibokusa Suwa Shrine Festival, held in the village of Oshino, near the foot of the mountain. This festival takes place in early May and is dedicated to the gods of Mount Fuji and the surrounding land. The festival includes traditional performances, such as taiko drumming and kagura dance, which are performed to honor the gods and ensure a good harvest for the coming year. The villagers also carry a portable shrine through the fields, offering prayers for fertility and protection from natural disasters. The festival is a joyful and vibrant event, filled with music, dancing, and prayers, and it reflects the deep connection that the people of Oshino feel with Mount Fuji and the natural world around them.

Throughout the year, there are many other smaller festivals and events that celebrate Mount Fuji's spiritual and cultural significance. Some of these festivals focus on the mountain's natural beauty, while others highlight its role in Japanese mythology and religion. For example, in early April, when the cherry blossoms are in full bloom, the area around Mount Fuji is filled with people celebrating the beauty of spring. Many towns and villages hold hanami (cherry blossom viewing) festivals, where people gather to admire the blossoms and enjoy picnics under the trees. With Mount Fuji in the background, the sight of cherry blossoms in full bloom is a breathtaking reminder of Japan's natural beauty and cultural heritage.

Another popular festival is the Mount Fuji Marathon, held every November in the town of Fujikawaguchiko. While this event is primarily a sporting event, it also has a strong cultural and spiritual element. The marathon route takes runners around the base of Mount Fuji and along the shores of the famous Fuji Five Lakes, offering stunning views of the mountain throughout the race. Many participants see the marathon as a way to challenge themselves physically and mentally, much like the pilgrims who climb the mountain. The marathon is also a celebration of the natural beauty of the region, and it brings together people from all over the world to experience the majesty of Mount Fuji.

These festivals and rituals reflect the deep reverence that the people of Japan have for Mount Fuji. Whether through traditional Shinto ceremonies, ancient pilgrimages, or modern sporting events, Mount Fuji continues to inspire awe and devotion. Its sacred status is not just a thing of the past—it remains a powerful symbol of Japan's spiritual and cultural identity. Each year, people gather to honor the mountain, offer prayers for protection, and celebrate the natural beauty that has captivated hearts for centuries. In this way, Mount Fuji remains a timeless source of inspiration and a central figure in the spiritual life of Japan.

Chapter 10: Weather Wonders at the Summit

At the very top of Mount Fuji, something special happens—something that can only be described as weather wonders. This mountain, Japan's tallest and one of its most majestic, has a peak that stretches so high into the sky that it feels like another world. The weather at the summit is unlike anything you'd experience in the towns and cities below. While it can be sunny and warm at the base, at the top, conditions can be completely different—extreme, ever-changing, and sometimes very unpredictable. These weather wonders make reaching the summit a unique and sometimes challenging experience for climbers and explorers.

One of the most interesting things about the summit of Mount Fuji is how cold it can get, even in the middle of summer. While it might be hot and humid down in Tokyo or at the base of the mountain, at the top, temperatures can drop dramatically. In fact, even in July and August, the warmest months, it's not uncommon for the temperature at the summit to fall below freezing at night. During the day, temperatures can hover around 5 to 7 degrees Celsius (about 40 to 45 degrees Fahrenheit), but when the sun sets, or if the clouds roll in, the chill in the air can be surprising. Climbers have to be prepared with warm clothing, even if they start their hike in shorts and a t-shirt, because the weather changes quickly as they climb higher and higher.

Speaking of clouds, they are a big part of the weather wonders at the summit. Sometimes, Mount Fuji's peak sits above the clouds, giving climbers the incredible experience of looking out over a sea of fluffy white clouds below them. It's a bit like being in an airplane, but without the windows. The feeling of standing on solid ground while gazing out over a world of clouds is breathtaking. On clear days, climbers can see for miles and miles—sometimes all the way to Tokyo, and on rare occasions, even to the ocean. But other times, the summit itself is swallowed by clouds. One moment, the sky is clear, and the next, thick clouds can roll in, reducing visibility to almost zero. When this happens, it's as if the mountain is wrapped in a blanket of mist, and everything feels mysterious and quiet.

The winds at the summit are another part of the weather wonders. Because Mount Fuji is so tall and stands alone without any other mountains nearby, it is exposed to strong winds, especially at the top. These winds can be incredibly powerful, sometimes reaching speeds of up to 100 kilometers per hour (about 62 miles per hour). For climbers, this means holding on to their hats and jackets, and sometimes even leaning into the wind just to stay upright. The wind can make the cold temperatures feel even colder, and when it's especially gusty, it can be difficult to move forward. But on calmer days, the wind can be refreshing, a cool breeze that adds to the feeling of being on top of the world.

One of the most magical weather phenomena at the summit of Mount Fuji is the sunrise. Climbing Mount Fuji to watch the sunrise is a tradition that goes back centuries, and it's easy to see why. The sunrise from the summit is called "Goraiko," which means "honorable sunrise." Many climbers begin their hike in the middle of the night so that they can reach the top just as the sun begins to rise. Watching the sky slowly change colors—from deep blues and purples to pinks, oranges, and golds—is an unforgettable experience. As the sun peeks over the horizon, its light spreads across the sky and bathes the mountain in a warm, golden glow. On a clear morning, the view is spectacular. But even if there are clouds, the sight of the sun's rays breaking through them can be just as breathtaking. The sunrise at the summit is so revered that some people consider it a spiritual experience, as if they are witnessing the birth of a new day from a place close to the heavens.

However, not all weather wonders at the summit are peaceful and serene. Thunderstorms can also occur, and they can be quite dangerous.

Being at such a high elevation during a storm means being very close to the thunder and lightning. When a storm rolls in, the thunder can feel like it's shaking the very ground beneath your feet, and the lightning seems to strike right next to the mountain. For safety reasons, climbers are advised to descend quickly if they see storm clouds forming. But even though thunderstorms can be scary, they also add to the sense of Mount Fuji being a place of immense power, where nature is in charge and humans are just visitors.

Another weather wonder that occurs at the summit is the formation of ice, even when it's not snowing. Because the air is so cold and the wind is so strong, moisture in the air can freeze onto the surfaces of rocks, signs, and even people's clothing. This frozen moisture is called rime ice, and it creates a sparkling, frosty landscape at the top of the mountain. Everything looks as if it's been dusted with a layer of sugar. The rime ice forms delicate patterns that glisten in the sunlight, turning the summit into a frozen wonderland. It's one of those magical sights that makes the difficult climb feel completely worth it.

In the winter months, Mount Fuji is completely covered in snow, and the summit becomes even more inhospitable. The temperatures can drop well below freezing, and the snow can pile up to several meters deep. While most people don't climb Mount Fuji in the winter due to the dangerous conditions, the mountain's appearance changes dramatically. From a distance, Mount Fuji looks like a perfect snow-capped cone, its white peak gleaming against the blue sky. The snow adds a sense of purity and majesty to the mountain, making it even more awe-inspiring.

One rare and special weather phenomenon that sometimes occurs at the summit is a cloud formation known as a "cap cloud" or "lenticular cloud." These clouds form when strong winds blow over the mountain, causing the air to rise and cool, creating a cloud that looks like a smooth, rounded cap sitting right on top of Mount Fuji's peak. Sometimes, the cap cloud looks like a flying saucer, hovering just above the mountain. It's a strange and beautiful sight, and it adds to the feeling that Mount Fuji is a place of magic and wonder. People who are lucky enough to see this phenomenon often feel as though they've witnessed something truly special.

In addition to these unique weather phenomena, the summit of Mount Fuji also experiences another interesting effect: lower oxygen levels. Because the summit is so high—about 3,776 meters (12,389 feet) above sea level—the air at the top is thinner, meaning there is less oxygen to breathe. Climbers often feel the effects of the altitude, experiencing symptoms like shortness of breath, dizziness, or fatigue. This is known as altitude sickness, and it can make the climb even more challenging. But for many, the feeling of being at such a high altitude, where the air is crisp and thin, adds to the excitement of reaching the summit.

Even though the weather at the summit of Mount Fuji can be unpredictable and sometimes harsh, it's also part of what makes the mountain so special. The ever-changing conditions keep climbers on their toes, reminding them that they are in a place where nature rules. Whether it's the freezing temperatures, the howling winds, the breathtaking sunrise, or the magical cloud formations, the weather at the summit of Mount Fuji is full of surprises. Each climber's experience is unique, and no two days at the top are ever the same. It's these weather wonders that make Mount Fuji not just a mountain, but a place of adventure, beauty, and awe.

Chapter 11: How Mount Fuji Became a UNESCO Site

Mount Fuji is not only Japan's tallest mountain and a national symbol, but it has also earned global recognition for its cultural and historical importance. In 2013, Mount Fuji was designated as a UNESCO World Heritage Site, which marked a significant milestone in its history. This prestigious status wasn't just awarded because of the mountain's natural beauty or impressive height. Instead, Mount Fuji became a UNESCO site due to its deep cultural, religious, and artistic significance to Japan and the world. The journey to becoming a UNESCO site is a long and fascinating story that reflects how much Mount Fuji means to the people of Japan and beyond.

The process of getting Mount Fuji recognized as a UNESCO World Heritage Site took many years of planning and effort. The mountain had long been cherished by the Japanese people, but there was a growing realization that its importance extended far beyond just being a stunning natural feature. Mount Fuji had inspired countless works of art, literature, and poetry, and it was also a place of pilgrimage and spiritual reflection. These cultural and spiritual elements were what made Fuji more than just a mountain, and they were key in helping it gain UNESCO recognition.

Before Mount Fuji could be considered for UNESCO status, there needed to be a clear case for why it should be included on the World Heritage List. UNESCO sites are chosen based on their "outstanding universal value," which means they need to be important not just to one country, but to all of humanity. Japan already had several UNESCO sites, such as ancient temples, castles, and historic villages, but Mount Fuji was something different. It wasn't a man-made structure; it was a natural landmark. However, what made Fuji unique was how much it had shaped Japanese culture, religion, and the arts for centuries.

One of the key aspects of Mount Fuji's bid for UNESCO status was its role as a sacred place. For over a thousand years, Mount Fuji has been a site of religious significance, especially in Shintoism, the indigenous religion of Japan, and Buddhism. Both Shinto and Buddhist practices are closely tied to nature, and Mount Fuji, with its majestic and powerful presence, became a spiritual icon. Pilgrims have climbed Mount Fuji for centuries as part of religious rituals, believing that reaching the summit would bring them closer to enlightenment or the gods. The mountain is considered a sacred being itself in Shinto beliefs, and many shrines dedicated to gods and spirits can be found in the area surrounding Fuji. The Fujisan Hongū Sengen Taisha, a Shinto shrine at the foot of the mountain, is one of the most important of these, and it's closely tied to the mountain's spiritual significance.

Buddhism also played a role in the cultural significance of Mount Fuji. In the 12th century, a sect of Japanese Buddhism called Fujiko emerged, and it focused on worshipping Mount Fuji. Followers believed that the mountain was a gateway to the afterlife, and they would make pilgrimages to Fuji's summit as a way to purify their spirits. Over time, climbing Fuji became more than just a religious act—it became a cultural tradition, one that connected people to the spiritual world as well as the natural one.

Another important factor in Mount Fuji's UNESCO designation was its influence on Japanese art and literature. Fuji's near-perfect cone shape and its towering presence above the surrounding landscape have made it a beloved subject for artists, poets, and writers throughout history. One of the most famous representations of Mount Fuji comes from the Edo period in the form of woodblock prints, particularly the works of Katsushika Hokusai and his series "Thirty-Six Views of Mount Fuji." Hokusai's prints, especially "The Great Wave off Kanagawa," became iconic images that not only celebrated the mountain's beauty but also represented the connection between nature and human life. These prints, along with many other depictions of

Mount Fuji in art, helped spread the image of Fuji around the world, turning it into a symbol of Japan itself.

Literature, too, has been greatly influenced by Mount Fuji. Throughout Japanese history, poets and writers have penned works inspired by the mountain's beauty and grandeur. Classical Japanese poetry, known as waka, often includes references to Fuji, describing it in various seasons, from its snow-capped peak in winter to its lush green slopes in summer. Mount Fuji has also featured in countless folktales and legends, further embedding it into the cultural imagination of Japan. This rich literary and artistic heritage was another reason why UNESCO recognized Fuji, as it showed how deeply the mountain had influenced Japanese culture for centuries.

As the application process for UNESCO status continued, one of the challenges was to protect Mount Fuji's natural environment while also recognizing its cultural and spiritual importance. The area around Mount Fuji had become a popular destination for tourists and climbers, and this had led to concerns about environmental degradation. Litter, erosion, and overcrowding were becoming problems, especially during the climbing season in the summer. In order to meet UNESCO's standards, Japan needed to ensure that the site would be protected for future generations. This led to efforts to clean up the mountain and manage the number of visitors, with programs put in place to reduce the environmental impact of tourism.

The Japanese government, along with local communities and religious organizations, worked together to present a strong case for Mount Fuji's UNESCO recognition. They emphasized not just the mountain's physical beauty, but also its deep connections to Japan's spiritual life, its artistic contributions, and its role in shaping the nation's identity. After years of preparation and effort, UNESCO officially designated Mount Fuji as a World Heritage Site in 2013, under the title "Fujisan, sacred place and source of artistic inspiration." This designation recognized the mountain's importance not just as a natural landmark, but as a symbol of cultural, religious, and artistic heritage.

Becoming a UNESCO World Heritage Site was a huge honor for Mount Fuji and for Japan as a whole. It meant that the mountain was now recognized as a place of universal value, one that belongs to all of humanity, not just to the people of Japan. This status has helped raise awareness about the need to protect and preserve Mount Fuji for future generations, ensuring that its natural beauty and cultural significance are respected.

Since becoming a UNESCO site, Mount Fuji has continued to attract visitors from around the world. Tourists, artists, climbers, and spiritual seekers all come to experience the mountain's unique power and beauty. Whether they are climbing to the summit to watch the sunrise, visiting one of the many shrines at its base, or simply admiring its shape from a distance, people are drawn to Fuji for many different reasons. But all of them share a sense of awe and respect for this incredible mountain, which has stood for thousands of years as a symbol of Japan's heart and soul.

Mount Fuji's journey to becoming a UNESCO World Heritage Site is a story of recognition—not just of its natural splendor, but of its deep cultural significance. It's a place where nature, spirituality, art, and history come together in a way that few other places on Earth can match. As a UNESCO site, Mount Fuji now has a special status that ensures it will be protected and cherished for many generations to come, allowing people from all over the world to experience its wonders, its stories, and its timeless beauty.

Chapter 12: The Forest at Fuji's Base

At the base of Mount Fuji lies a forest that is as intriguing as it is mysterious. This forest, called Aokigahara, is sometimes referred to as the "Sea of Trees" because its thick canopy of trees makes it appear like a rolling sea of green from a distance. The forest covers a large area, spreading across the northwestern foot of the mountain, and has a unique and captivating atmosphere that draws visitors from all over the world. But Aokigahara is more than just a dense, quiet woodland; it is a place filled with fascinating natural features, local legends, and historical significance. Exploring the forest around Fuji's base is like stepping into another world, where nature, history, and mystery are intertwined.

Aokigahara's origins are tied to Mount Fuji's volcanic past. Around 1,100 years ago, a massive eruption of Mount Fuji occurred, spewing lava and ash across the surrounding land. As the lava cooled and hardened, it formed the foundation for what would become the Aokigahara forest. Over centuries, plants and trees began to grow on the rocky terrain, slowly transforming it into the lush forest we see today. Because of the lava bed that lies underneath, the forest floor is uneven and rugged in places, with cracks and crevices that add to the eerie, otherworldly feel of the landscape.

One of the most interesting aspects of Aokigahara is its unique ecosystem. The forest is home to a wide variety of plant species, some of which thrive in the nutrient-poor volcanic soil. Moss, ferns, and shrubs grow abundantly, covering the forest floor in a thick, green carpet. The trees in Aokigahara, mainly evergreen species like Japanese cypress, hemlock, and fir, grow tall and close together, creating a canopy that blocks out much of the sunlight. This thick canopy makes the forest feel darker and quieter than other woodlands, and the dense foliage dampens sound, adding to the sense of isolation. Visitors often remark that Aokigahara feels strangely silent, as if the forest itself is holding its breath.

Despite its quiet and stillness, Aokigahara is full of life. Animals such as wild boars, deer, and small mammals make their home in the forest, and a wide variety of birds can be heard chirping in the trees. Insects also thrive here, with butterflies, beetles, and other small creatures adding to the forest's biodiversity. The forest's natural beauty, with its towering trees, moss-covered rocks, and peaceful atmosphere, makes it a popular spot for hikers and nature lovers who come to experience its tranquility.

However, Aokigahara's appeal goes beyond its natural beauty. The forest has long been a place of mystery and legend in Japanese culture. For centuries, it has been associated with the supernatural, and many people believe that it is haunted by spirits. These beliefs likely stem from the forest's history and the fact that it is so different from other woodlands. The thick trees, uneven ground, and maze-like trails make it easy to get lost in Aokigahara, and there are many stories of people wandering into the forest and never coming back.

One of the most famous legends surrounding Aokigahara is that it is haunted by the yūrei, which are spirits of the dead in Japanese folklore. According to tradition, yūrei are souls who have died with unresolved feelings, such as anger, sadness, or regret, and they are believed to roam the earth until they can find peace. Because of this, Aokigahara is sometimes called the "suicide forest" due to the unfortunate history of people going there to end their lives. These tragic events have only deepened the sense of mystery and fear that surrounds the forest. Local myths say that the spirits of those who have died there linger in the trees, adding to the forest's reputation as a haunted place.

Despite these eerie stories, many people visit Aokigahara for peaceful and meditative purposes. The forest is part of Fuji-Hakone-Izu National Park, and it has several walking trails that allow visitors to explore its natural wonders safely. Hikers can take in the forest's quiet beauty while walking along the paths, enjoying the cool shade of the trees and the soothing sounds of nature. Along the way, visitors can see interesting geological features, such as lava tubes and caves that formed during Mount Fuji's volcanic eruptions. Some of these caves, like the Narusawa Ice Cave and the Fugaku Wind Cave, are popular attractions and offer a glimpse into the volcanic forces that shaped the region.

The Narusawa Ice Cave, for example, is a fascinating underground tunnel that remains cold enough to keep ice frozen year-round. Visitors can walk through the cave and see the natural ice formations, even in the middle of summer. The Fugaku Wind Cave, on the other hand, was historically used to store silk cocoons because of its constant cool temperature. These caves, along with the unique lava formations on the forest floor, give visitors a sense of the powerful natural forces that created both Mount Fuji and Aokigahara.

In addition to its natural beauty, Aokigahara holds cultural significance as well. Throughout history, Mount Fuji and its surrounding forests have been considered sacred places in Japanese religion, particularly in Shintoism. The forest is part of the larger spiritual landscape of Mount Fuji, which has been a destination for pilgrims and worshippers for centuries. Many believe that the mountain and its forests are home to kami, or spirits, who watch over the land. Shrines dedicated to these spirits can be found around the base of Mount Fuji, and the forest itself is sometimes visited by those seeking spiritual reflection and connection with nature.

While Aokigahara is often viewed through the lens of its darker associations, it is important to remember that it is also a place of incredible natural beauty and wonder. The forest is a reminder of the power of nature, shaped by the eruptions of Mount Fuji and transformed over centuries into a thriving ecosystem. Its dense, quiet woods offer a place of solitude and reflection, where visitors can disconnect from the outside world and immerse themselves in the serene, green sea of trees.

Today, efforts are being made to preserve the forest and protect its natural environment. Because Aokigahara attracts many visitors, there are concerns about the impact of tourism on the forest's delicate ecosystem. Litter, erosion, and damage to plant life are all issues that conservationists are working to address. Visitors are encouraged to stay on the marked trails and follow the guidelines set by the national park to ensure that the forest remains a place of beauty for future generations.

In conclusion, the forest at Fuji's base, Aokigahara, is a place of contrasts. It is a lush, peaceful woodland that offers a haven for wildlife and a retreat for those seeking solitude, yet it is also a place steeped in mystery and folklore. Its volcanic origins, dense trees, and eerie silence give it an otherworldly feel, while its caves and lava formations remind visitors of the powerful forces that shaped it. Whether people visit for its natural beauty, its cultural significance, or its enigmatic history, Aokigahara is a place that leaves a lasting impression on all who explore its depths. The forest is not just a part of Mount Fuji's landscape, but a part of its soul—a place where the natural and the supernatural meet, and where the quiet majesty of the trees tells a story of time, mystery, and life.

Chapter 13: Volcanic Secrets Beneath Mount Fuji

Beneath the surface of Mount Fuji lies a hidden world that holds the secrets of one of the most famous and majestic volcanoes on Earth. Although Mount Fuji is renowned for its towering beauty, it is also an active volcano, and much of its history, power, and potential are hidden deep beneath its surface. Understanding the volcanic secrets beneath Mount Fuji requires a dive into the mountain's geological past, its complex structure, and the volcanic forces that shaped it. While the mountain has stood for thousands of years, the hidden activities beneath its surface continue to shape both its future and the land around it.

Mount Fuji is a stratovolcano, which means it is built up in layers over time from repeated eruptions of lava, ash, and other volcanic materials. These layers give Fuji its iconic symmetrical shape, but they also tell the story of the volcano's long and complicated life. Underneath its peaceful, snow-capped peak, Mount Fuji's underground structure is like a patchwork of hardened lava flows, ancient volcanic debris, and hidden magma chambers that stretch far below the surface. These magma chambers hold molten rock, or magma, which is the source of Fuji's volcanic power. When the pressure in these chambers builds up, it can force the magma to the surface, causing an eruption.

To truly appreciate the volcanic secrets beneath Mount Fuji, it's important to go back in time to understand how the volcano was formed. Mount Fuji is actually the latest in a series of volcanic mountains that have formed in this region over millions of years. Scientists believe that before Mount Fuji appeared, there were at least two older volcanoes in the same location. These ancient volcanoes, known as Komitake and Ko-Fuji, erupted and built up large volcanic mountains, but over time, their activity slowed and they became dormant. Mount Fuji, which began to form around 100,000 years ago, eventually rose above these older volcanoes, creating the majestic peak we see today.

The formation of Mount Fuji involved multiple stages of volcanic activity. During the earliest stage, lava flows from the new Fuji volcano covered the remains of the older Ko-Fuji volcano, forming the base of the mountain. As the eruptions continued, ash, pumice, and other materials from explosive eruptions added to the growing mountain, building it layer by layer. This process of alternating quiet lava flows and more violent explosive eruptions is what gave Mount Fuji its classic cone shape. The current Fuji, known as "Shin-Fuji" or "New Fuji," is the result of thousands of years of volcanic activity.

Beneath the surface, the forces that created Mount Fuji are still at work. Deep underground, molten rock from the Earth's mantle pushes upward through cracks and weaknesses in the Earth's crust. These movements of magma are driven by tectonic activity, as Japan lies at the boundary of several tectonic plates. The Pacific Plate, the Philippine Sea Plate, and the Eurasian Plate are constantly shifting and colliding with each other, and this tectonic activity creates the perfect conditions for volcanic eruptions. The pressure created by these moving plates causes magma to rise toward the surface, and when that pressure becomes too great, it results in an eruption.

One of the most fascinating volcanic secrets beneath Mount Fuji is the presence of its vast and complex magma chamber system. These chambers act like underground reservoirs, holding magma until it is ready to erupt. However, not all magma makes it to the surface in the form of an eruption. Some magma remains trapped deep within the Earth, slowly cooling and hardening into solid rock. Over time, these layers of cooled magma become part of the mountain's structure, contributing to the layers of volcanic rock that make up Mount Fuji.

While Mount Fuji has been relatively quiet for the past few centuries, scientists closely monitor the volcanic activity beneath the mountain. Using advanced technology such as seismographs and GPS instruments, they can detect even the slightest movements in the Earth's crust and changes in the shape of the mountain. These instruments help scientists keep track of any signs that magma is rising toward the surface, which could indicate the possibility of an eruption. Seismic activity, or the shaking caused by movements of the Earth's crust, is one of the key indicators that an eruption may be imminent. By studying the patterns of earthquakes and tremors beneath Mount Fuji, scientists can learn more about the volcanic activity happening deep below the surface.

In addition to monitoring seismic activity, scientists also study the gases that escape from Mount Fuji's vents and fissures. Volcanic gases, such as carbon dioxide and sulfur dioxide, are released as magma rises toward the surface. By analyzing the levels of these gases, scientists can get clues about what is happening inside the volcano. For example, an increase in the amount of sulfur dioxide might suggest that magma is getting closer to the surface and that an eruption could be on the horizon.

One of the most intriguing questions that scientists continue to explore is whether Mount Fuji is building up toward another major eruption. Although the last eruption occurred in 1707, known as the Hoei eruption, Mount Fuji is still classified as an active volcano. This means that it has the potential to erupt again in the future. The Hoei eruption was particularly powerful, sending ash and volcanic debris as far as Edo (modern-day Tokyo), over 100 kilometers away. While Mount Fuji has remained quiet since then, its underground magma chambers are still active, and the forces that could trigger another eruption are still present.

One of the challenges in predicting future eruptions is that every volcano behaves differently, and Mount Fuji is no exception. Volcanic activity is influenced by a variety of factors, including the composition of the magma, the pressure inside the magma chambers, and the tectonic activity in the region. While scientists have developed models to predict how Mount Fuji might behave in the future, there are still many unknowns. The mountain's underground structure is so complex that it's difficult to know exactly when or how it might erupt again.

In recent years, there has been growing concern about the potential impact of a future eruption of Mount Fuji on the surrounding region. Japan is one of the most densely populated countries in the world, and the area around Mount Fuji is home to millions of people. A major eruption could have devastating consequences, not only for the nearby towns and cities but also for the economy and infrastructure of the entire country. The ash and volcanic debris from an eruption could disrupt air travel, damage buildings, and cause widespread power outages. In addition, the volcanic gases released during an eruption could pose serious health risks to people living in the area.

To prepare for the possibility of an eruption, the Japanese government has developed emergency plans and conducted drills to ensure that people living near Mount Fuji know how to respond in the event of a volcanic disaster. These plans include evacuation routes, shelters, and early warning systems to alert residents if an eruption is imminent. Scientists continue to study the volcano closely, using the latest technology to monitor its activity and improve their ability to predict future eruptions.

Despite the risks, Mount Fuji's volcanic activity is also a source of fascination and wonder. The mountain's eruptions over the centuries have played a major role in shaping the landscape of Japan and have created some of the country's most stunning natural features. For example, the Fuji Five Lakes, located at the base of the mountain, were formed by past eruptions that blocked rivers and created natural dams. These lakes are now popular tourist destinations, offering breathtaking views of Mount Fuji reflected in the water.

Mount Fuji's volcanic past has also contributed to its cultural and spiritual significance. The mountain has been considered a sacred place for centuries, and its volcanic power is seen as a symbol of both creation and destruction. In Japanese mythology, Mount Fuji is often associated with fire and the gods, and its eruptions are viewed as a reminder of the forces of nature that shape the world. Even today, Mount Fuji is a place of pilgrimage for many people, who come to hike its slopes and pay their respects to the mountain's spiritual power.

In conclusion, the volcanic secrets beneath Mount Fuji reveal a complex and dynamic system that has been shaping the landscape of Japan for thousands of years. From its ancient magma chambers to the tectonic forces driving its eruptions, Mount Fuji is a powerful reminder of the Earth's inner workings. While the mountain appears calm on the surface, its hidden volcanic activity continues to play a crucial role in the lives of the people living nearby. By studying these volcanic secrets, scientists hope to better understand the future of Mount Fuji and ensure the safety of those who live in its shadow. The story of Mount Fuji is one of awe-inspiring beauty and raw natural power, with its volcanic secrets still waiting to be fully uncovered.

Chapter 14: Mount Fuji in Famous Japanese Stories

Mount Fuji, with its towering peak and graceful presence, has been a source of inspiration for centuries. It stands as more than just a mountain; it represents beauty, strength, and mystery in Japanese culture. For thousands of years, storytellers have woven Mount Fuji into famous legends, folktales, and myths, making it a central figure in the imagination of the people. These stories, which have been passed down through generations, help explain why Mount Fuji is so revered and holds a special place in the hearts of the Japanese.

One of the most famous tales involving Mount Fuji is the story of the bamboo cutter and the Moon Princess, known as "The Tale of the Bamboo Cutter" or "The Tale of Princess Kaguya." This ancient story, believed to be one of the oldest in Japanese literature, tells the tale of a mysterious princess who was discovered inside a glowing bamboo stalk by an old bamboo cutter. The old man and his wife, who had no children, were overjoyed and raised the tiny princess as their own. As she grew, Princess Kaguya's beauty became legendary, and many noblemen came from far and wide to ask for her hand in marriage. However, Princess Kaguya set impossible tasks for her suitors, sending them on dangerous and unrealistic quests, and none were able to win her heart.

As time passed, Princess Kaguya revealed to her adoptive parents that she was not of this world but had come from the Moon. She was destined to return to her celestial home, despite the deep love she felt for her earthly parents. When the time came for her to return to the Moon, Princess Kaguya left behind a letter and a vial of elixir of immortality for the emperor, who had fallen in love with her but could not keep her on Earth. Heartbroken, the emperor took the letter and the elixir to the summit of Mount Fuji, where he burned them in hopes that the smoke would carry his feelings to the heavens. According to legend, this is why smoke used to rise from Mount Fuji's peak, a symbol of the emperor's unending love for the Moon Princess. This story has been cherished for centuries and is one of the reasons Mount Fuji is seen as a connection between the earthly and the divine.

Another famous legend associated with Mount Fuji is the tale of "Fuji no Yama," or "The Mountain of Immortality." This story speaks to the mountain's spiritual significance and its role as a symbol of eternal life. According to the legend, a powerful and wise emperor, Qin Shi Huang of China, sought the secret to immortality and sent an expedition of explorers to Japan to find it. The explorers traveled far and wide, eventually reaching Mount Fuji. Believing that the mountain held the key to eternal life due to its majestic and eternal appearance, they sought to make offerings to appease the gods who resided there. However, despite their efforts, they could not obtain the secret to immortality. Instead, Mount Fuji became a symbol of the eternal power of nature and the idea that some things in life, like death and the cycles of nature, cannot be changed or controlled by human desires. This story reflects how Mount Fuji has long been associated with immortality, not just in the physical sense but also in the idea of spiritual endurance and the lasting power of nature.

Mount Fuji also appears in countless ghost stories and supernatural tales, where the mountain is seen as both a place of beauty and mystery. In one such story, Mount Fuji is home to the goddess Konohanasakuya-hime, often called the Goddess of Mount Fuji. She is a deity of nature, particularly of flowers, and is believed to control the fertility of the land. According to legend, Konohanasakuya-hime was married to the god Ninigi, a descendant of the Sun Goddess Amaterasu. After their marriage, the goddess became pregnant, but Ninigi doubted her faithfulness, suspecting that her child was not his. To prove her loyalty and innocence, Konohanasakuya-hime entered a burning hut, declaring that if her child were truly Ninigi's, she and the baby would survive the flames. Miraculously, she gave birth to three children in the midst of the fire, unharmed, proving her fidelity. This story is one of many that associate Mount Fuji with purity, strength, and the resilience of nature, and Konohanasakuya-hime remains a beloved figure in Japanese mythology.

Many samurai legends also revolve around Mount Fuji, as the mountain was often seen as a symbol of bravery, honor, and the unshakable spirit of the warrior class. One such tale involves the famous samurai Minamoto no Yoritomo, the founder of the Kamakura shogunate. During his campaigns to unite Japan, Yoritomo is said to have prayed to the gods at Mount Fuji for strength and success in battle. According to legend, he received a vision from the mountain itself, granting him the courage and strategy needed to win his battles and bring peace to the land. This connection between Mount Fuji and the samurai spirit of perseverance and determination has made the mountain a symbol of strength in the face of adversity.

Another samurai-related story is about the renowned swordsman Miyamoto Musashi, who is said to have trained in the shadow of Mount Fuji. Musashi is known for his unmatched skill in swordsmanship and his philosophy of combat, and according to legend, he would climb Mount Fuji to meditate and train his mind as well as his body. The serene and powerful presence of the mountain was believed to help him sharpen his focus and prepare for the many duels and battles he would face. Musashi's connection to Mount Fuji is symbolic of the way in which the mountain has always been seen as a source of wisdom, strength, and spiritual growth for those who seek it.

In addition to its place in mythology and samurai legends, Mount Fuji has also been a central figure in Japanese literature and poetry for centuries. The famous haiku poet Matsuo Basho often wrote about Mount Fuji, capturing its beauty and grandeur in his short, evocative poems. In one haiku, Basho describes the sight of Mount Fuji reflected in the waters of a lake, capturing the peaceful and awe-inspiring feeling that the mountain evokes in those who see it. Other poets have written about the way Mount Fuji changes with the seasons, from its snow-capped peak in winter to the blooming flowers at its base in spring. The mountain has long been a symbol of the changing seasons and the cycles of life in Japanese poetry and art.

In Japanese art, Mount Fuji has been depicted countless times, but perhaps the most famous artistic representation of the mountain is in the woodblock print series "Thirty-Six Views of Mount Fuji" by the artist Katsushika Hokusai. Created in the early 19th century, this series of prints shows Mount Fuji from various angles and during different times of the year, highlighting the mountain's beauty and its central place in Japanese culture. The most famous print in the series, "The Great Wave off Kanagawa," shows a towering wave about to crash down on boats, with Mount Fuji calmly rising in the background. This image has become iconic not only in Japan but around the world, symbolizing the contrast between the power of nature and the unshakable presence of the mountain.

Mount Fuji has also appeared in numerous modern stories, films, and even video games, where it continues to serve as a symbol of Japan's cultural identity and natural beauty. In many films, Mount Fuji is depicted as a place of pilgrimage or a destination for characters seeking wisdom, strength, or a deeper understanding of themselves. The mountain's serene presence and its connection to Japanese history and mythology make it a perfect setting for stories about personal growth and transformation.

In conclusion, Mount Fuji is much more than a physical mountain. It is deeply embedded in the stories, legends, and culture of Japan. From ancient myths about goddesses and princesses to tales of samurai bravery and artistic masterpieces, Mount Fuji has inspired countless works of creativity and imagination. Its presence in famous Japanese stories reflects the deep connection between the people of Japan and the natural world around them, as well as their respect for the power and mystery of the forces that shape their lives. Through these stories, Mount Fuji remains not only a symbol of Japan but also a source of inspiration, hope, and spiritual significance for generations past, present, and future.

Chapter 15: Mount Fuji's Role in Modern Japan

Mount Fuji, Japan's tallest and most iconic mountain, plays a unique and profound role in modern Japan, blending tradition with contemporary life. As a symbol of beauty, strength, and cultural identity, Mount Fuji has evolved over the centuries from a sacred site revered in ancient mythology to a modern-day landmark that continues to influence Japanese society in many ways. Despite its ancient roots, Mount Fuji is not just a relic of the past; it remains deeply woven into the fabric of Japan's modern culture, economy, and way of life.

One of the most significant ways Mount Fuji influences modern Japan is through its status as a national symbol. Even though Japan is home to many famous landmarks and historical sites, none hold quite the same power or presence as Mount Fuji. It is a symbol of the country's natural beauty and its connection to both tradition and progress. The mountain is featured in countless representations across Japanese media, from the logos of companies to public art, and even on Japanese currency. The 1,000 yen bill, for example, prominently features an image of Mount Fuji, highlighting its significance as a national icon. In many ways, it represents the balance between nature and the hustle and bustle of Japan's rapidly modernizing cities.

In modern times, Mount Fuji also plays a critical role in Japan's tourism industry. Every year, millions of people from all over the world travel to see this majestic mountain with their own eyes. For many, climbing Mount Fuji is seen as a once-in-a-lifetime experience, a journey that connects them to the history, culture, and spirituality of Japan. The official climbing season takes place in the summer months, typically from July to September, when the weather is most favorable for trekkers. During this time, thousands of climbers set out each day to reach the summit, eager to see the sunrise from the top, a sight that is often referred to as the "Goraiko," which translates to "arrival of light." This sunrise view from Mount Fuji is considered so beautiful and spiritually significant that it draws climbers not only from Japan but from across the globe. Even those who do not climb Mount Fuji often visit the area to see the mountain's snow-capped peak or to enjoy the natural beauty surrounding the mountain.

Aside from tourism, Mount Fuji has a direct economic impact on the surrounding region. The areas around the base of Mount Fuji, including the Five Lakes region, are home to a number of resorts, hotels, and recreational facilities that cater to visitors looking to explore the natural beauty of the area. The local economy thrives on the influx of tourists who come to experience the mountain's beauty, visit its hot springs, or enjoy outdoor activities like hiking, boating, and fishing. Numerous souvenir shops, restaurants, and traditional inns (known as ryokan) offer visitors a taste of Japanese culture while they take in the breathtaking views of the mountain. This steady flow of tourism helps support jobs and businesses in the region, making Mount Fuji not just a natural wonder but also a vital economic resource.

Modern technology has also enhanced Mount Fuji's role in Japan. The mountain is frequently featured in television shows, movies, commercials, and even anime and video games. Its image is instantly recognizable and often used to evoke feelings of nostalgia, pride, and the enduring connection between Japan's past and present. Thanks to modern photography and drone technology, stunning images and aerial videos of Mount Fuji are more accessible than ever before, allowing people worldwide to experience the mountain's beauty from the comfort of their homes. Social media platforms like Instagram and YouTube are filled with breathtaking photos and videos of Mount Fuji, further cementing its status as a global icon.

Mount Fuji's role in Japanese art and culture has also evolved in modern times. While it has long been a subject of traditional Japanese art, particularly in woodblock prints like Katsushika Hokusai's famous "Thirty-Six Views of Mount Fuji," contemporary artists and designers continue to be inspired by the mountain. Mount Fuji's distinctive shape and serene presence make it a popular subject in modern art forms, including painting, sculpture, and digital media. Many contemporary Japanese artists incorporate Mount Fuji into their works, often using it as a symbol of the enduring beauty of nature in the face of modern urbanization and industrialization. This connection between Mount Fuji and modern art allows the mountain to maintain its cultural relevance in a rapidly changing world.

In addition to its cultural significance, Mount Fuji also plays an important role in Japanese environmental and conservation efforts. Recognizing the need to protect the natural beauty of the mountain and its surrounding ecosystems, the Japanese government, along with various environmental organizations, has worked to ensure that Mount Fuji remains a pristine natural environment for future generations. One of the key challenges in recent years has been managing the impact of mass tourism on the mountain's delicate ecosystem. To address this, several initiatives have been put in place, including stricter waste management policies, designated hiking routes to minimize environmental damage, and efforts to educate visitors on the importance of preserving the natural environment. These conservation efforts reflect the growing awareness in modern Japan of the need to balance the preservation of natural wonders like Mount Fuji with the demands of tourism and economic development.

Modern Japan also continues to celebrate Mount Fuji through various festivals and cultural events. These festivals often combine traditional religious practices with modern celebrations, demonstrating how Mount Fuji continues to bridge the gap between Japan's past and present. One such event is the Fuji Shibazakura Festival, held each spring near the base of the mountain. During the festival, thousands of colorful pink moss flowers, known as shibazakura, bloom in the fields around Mount Fuji, creating a breathtaking scene with the mountain as a backdrop. The festival attracts visitors from all over Japan and beyond, who come to enjoy the beauty of the flowers and the majestic view of Mount Fuji in the distance. The combination of natural beauty and cultural celebration helps to keep Mount Fuji's legacy alive in the hearts of the Japanese people.

Furthermore, Mount Fuji has come to symbolize not only the natural beauty of Japan but also its spiritual and philosophical values. The mountain remains a site of pilgrimage for many who seek spiritual enlightenment or personal growth. While the religious significance of Mount Fuji is rooted in ancient traditions, such as Shinto and Buddhism, its role as a place of reflection and self-discovery continues to resonate in modern Japan. Many people who climb Mount Fuji today do so not just for the physical challenge but also as a way to connect with nature and find inner peace. The mountain's quiet strength and imposing presence serve as a reminder of the power of nature and the importance of maintaining balance in one's life.

In modern literature and pop culture, Mount Fuji continues to be a popular theme. Japanese authors and poets frequently reference the mountain in their works, using it as a metaphor for beauty, endurance, and the challenges of life. Likewise, Mount Fuji appears in countless films, television shows, and advertisements, both in Japan and internationally. Its image is often used to evoke a sense of calm or wonder, and it has become a symbol not just of Japan but of the larger world's fascination with the natural beauty and cultural heritage of the country.

Mount Fuji has even extended its influence into the realm of science and research. Because of its geological significance as a dormant volcano, Mount Fuji is closely studied by scientists who seek to understand the mountain's volcanic history and potential future activity. Advanced monitoring systems have been installed on the mountain to track seismic activity and volcanic gas emissions, helping researchers gather valuable data that could be used to predict and prepare for any future eruptions. This scientific interest in Mount Fuji highlights the mountain's importance not just as a cultural and spiritual icon but also as a significant natural feature with global scientific relevance.

In conclusion, Mount Fuji's role in modern Japan is multifaceted and dynamic. It remains a symbol of national pride and cultural identity, representing the beauty of nature and the enduring strength of the Japanese people. Its influence extends beyond the physical mountain, touching nearly every aspect of Japanese society, from tourism and the economy to art, literature, and spirituality. Despite the rapid modernization of Japan, Mount Fuji continues to stand as a timeless symbol, connecting the past with the present and reminding people of the natural and cultural treasures that define the country. As Japan continues to grow and evolve, Mount Fuji will undoubtedly remain a central figure in the nation's heart, inspiring generations to come with its majestic presence and profound significance.

Chapter 16: The Geology Behind Mount Fuji's Formation

Mount Fuji is not only a symbol of Japan's cultural heritage but also a geological marvel that has intrigued scientists and geologists for centuries. Its formation, spanning hundreds of thousands of years, is a testament to the powerful forces that shape our planet. Mount Fuji's towering peak, with its nearly symmetrical cone, is the result of complex volcanic activity that continues to this day. To truly understand Mount Fuji, we must dive deep into the layers of its geological history, exploring the processes that gave rise to one of the world's most famous volcanoes.

Mount Fuji, located near the boundary of three tectonic plates—the Eurasian Plate, the Philippine Sea Plate, and the North American Plate—was formed by volcanic activity that occurred at the intersection of these plates. The movement of tectonic plates is one of the most fundamental forces driving geological change on Earth. As these plates move, they interact with each other, sometimes colliding, pulling apart, or sliding past one another. In the case of Mount Fuji, it lies in a region where the Philippine Sea Plate is being pushed underneath the Eurasian Plate in a process known as subduction.

Subduction zones are key areas for volcanic activity. As one plate is forced beneath another, it sinks into the Earth's mantle, where the immense heat and pressure cause it to melt, generating magma. This molten rock can then rise toward the surface, eventually erupting to form a volcano. Mount Fuji's origins are tied to this process, but its story is far from simple. In fact, the mountain we see today is the result of not just one, but multiple volcanic stages that have built up over time, each contributing to the mountain's iconic shape.

The first stage of Mount Fuji's formation began about 700,000 years ago, when an older volcano, known as the Komitake Volcano, erupted. Komitake was a stratovolcano, meaning it was built up by layers of hardened lava, ash, and volcanic rock over time. Stratovolcanoes, which include some of the most famous volcanoes in the world, are characterized by their steep, conical shapes, and Komitake was no exception. However, while the Komitake Volcano laid the initial groundwork, it would not be recognizable as the Mount Fuji we know today.

After Komitake, another volcanic phase began about 100,000 years ago. This was the beginning of what geologists call "Old Fuji." During this time, a new volcanic cone started to grow atop the remains of the older Komitake Volcano. Lava flowed from the Earth's crust, piling up layer by layer, and frequent eruptions helped shape the cone that would eventually become the base of Mount Fuji. The volcanic activity of Old Fuji was intense, with frequent eruptions of both lava and ash, creating a stratovolcano much larger than the earlier Komitake.

The transformation from Old Fuji to the Mount Fuji we recognize today occurred about 10,000 years ago, during what is known as the "New Fuji" stage. This period marked the most recent and significant phase of volcanic activity. The eruptions during this time were explosive, and the layers of lava and ash deposited over millennia created the steep, smooth slopes of the modern mountain. The cone that emerged during this period is what gives Mount Fuji its near-perfect symmetry and striking appearance. The eruptions of New Fuji have continued into recorded history, with the most recent major eruption occurring in 1707.

This 1707 eruption, known as the Hoei Eruption, is one of the most famous volcanic events in Japan's history. It began with a violent explosion that sent ash and rocks high into the sky. Over the course of several weeks, large amounts of ash and volcanic debris covered the surrounding areas, even reaching as far as Edo (modern-day Tokyo), which is over 100 kilometers away. The Hoei Eruption created a secondary crater on the southeastern side of Mount Fuji, known as the

Hoei Crater, which can still be seen today. This eruption was significant because, unlike many of Mount Fuji's previous eruptions, it did not produce much lava. Instead, it was a primarily explosive eruption that covered the land in ash and pumice, disrupting agriculture and daily life in the region.

While Mount Fuji has not erupted since the Hoei Eruption, it is still considered an active volcano. Geologists continue to monitor the mountain closely for signs of volcanic activity. The region is equipped with sensors that track seismic activity, gas emissions, and other indicators that could signal an impending eruption. Because Mount Fuji is located near densely populated areas, including Tokyo, any future eruptions could have serious consequences, making it one of the most closely watched volcanoes in the world.

One of the key features of Mount Fuji's geology is its stratovolcano structure. As mentioned earlier, stratovolcanoes are built up from layers of lava flows, volcanic ash, and other debris. This type of volcano tends to produce eruptions that are both explosive and effusive, meaning that they can release both volcanic ash and lava. The alternating layers of lava and ash create a strong, stable structure, allowing the volcano to grow taller over time. Mount Fuji's symmetrical shape is the result of this steady build-up of layers, with lava flows smoothing out the cone's surface.

The composition of Mount Fuji's lava is also a crucial factor in its formation. The lava that erupts from Mount Fuji is primarily basalt, a type of volcanic rock that is relatively low in silica content. Basaltic lava tends to be less viscous (or thick) than other types of lava, allowing it to flow more easily. This characteristic is one of the reasons why Mount Fuji has such smooth, flowing slopes. When the basaltic lava erupts, it spreads out over a wide area before cooling and hardening, creating the gently sloping base that gives Mount Fuji its graceful appearance.

Beneath the surface, the geological activity that fuels Mount Fuji's eruptions is driven by the intense heat and pressure of the Earth's mantle. The mantle is the layer of rock beneath the Earth's crust, and it is constantly in motion due to the immense heat generated by the planet's core. In subduction zones like the one near Mount Fuji, the sinking tectonic plates create a melting zone in the mantle, where rock is heated to the point of becoming magma. This magma rises toward the surface, collecting in magma chambers beneath the volcano. When enough pressure builds up, the magma forces its way through cracks in the Earth's crust, leading to an eruption.

One of the fascinating aspects of Mount Fuji's geology is the way it has influenced the surrounding landscape. The repeated eruptions over the millennia have created a variety of geological features, including lava flows, volcanic plateaus, and volcanic caves. The lava flows from past eruptions have shaped the terrain around the mountain, creating fertile soil that supports lush forests and agriculture. In addition to the natural beauty of the landscape, these geological features provide important clues for scientists studying the history and future potential of volcanic activity in the region.

Mount Fuji's geology is also closely tied to the region's water systems. The mountain plays a critical role in the local hydrology, with its snow-capped peak acting as a source of fresh water. Each winter, snow accumulates on Mount Fuji's summit, and when the snow melts in the spring and summer, the water seeps into the ground, feeding rivers, lakes, and underground aquifers. This water is essential for both human consumption and agriculture in the surrounding areas. The five lakes at the base of Mount Fuji—Lake Kawaguchi, Lake Yamanaka, Lake Sai, Lake Shoji, and Lake Motosu—are all part of this water system, and they provide important resources for the region's inhabitants.

In recent years, scientific studies have revealed even more about the volcanic secrets hidden beneath Mount Fuji. Geophysical surveys have shown that there are multiple layers of magma chambers beneath the mountain, suggesting that the volcano has the potential for future eruptions. These magma chambers are located at different depths, with some as deep as 20 kilometers below the surface. The deeper magma chambers are likely connected to the subduction process that originally formed Mount Fuji, while the shallower chambers are thought to be responsible for the more recent volcanic activity.

Geologists continue to study Mount Fuji's magma system, using advanced technologies like seismic tomography and GPS monitoring to track changes in the Earth's crust. By analyzing the movement of magma beneath the surface, scientists can gain valuable insights into the potential for future eruptions. While there is no way to predict exactly when or if Mount Fuji will erupt again, this ongoing research helps to improve our understanding of the mountain's geological behavior and the risks it may pose to the surrounding region.

In conclusion, the geology behind Mount Fuji's formation is a story of immense natural forces shaping one of the world's most iconic landscapes. From its origins in the subduction of tectonic plates to its growth through countless volcanic eruptions, Mount Fuji is a living reminder of the power of Earth's geology. Its stratovolcano structure, basaltic lava flows, and ongoing volcanic activity make it a unique and fascinating subject of study. As both a symbol of Japan and a geological wonder, Mount Fuji continues to captivate scientists, tourists, and residents alike, standing as a testament to the dynamic processes that shape our planet.

Chapter 17: Famous Explorers of Mount Fuji

Mount Fuji has long been a destination of fascination, not only for those who live in its shadow but for people from around the world. While the mountain itself holds deep spiritual significance for the Japanese people, its imposing height and beauty have also captured the attention of adventurers, explorers, and mountaineers for centuries. The story of the famous explorers who dared to climb Mount Fuji is filled with bravery, determination, and a desire to reach the summit of Japan's most iconic peak. Each of these explorers played a key role in unraveling the mysteries of Fuji, and their expeditions have become legendary in the history of mountaineering.

Mount Fuji has been climbed for well over a thousand years, but many early explorers were not simply adventurers—they were pilgrims. For centuries, religious pilgrims made the journey to Mount Fuji's summit, believing it to be a sacred site. These early climbers were often monks or followers of the Shinto and Buddhist faiths who saw the mountain as a pathway to enlightenment. One of the most famous early explorers of Mount Fuji was En no Gyōja, a legendary ascetic and mountain hermit who is said to have climbed Fuji in the 7th century. He was known for his deep connection to nature and for practicing Shugendō, a form of Japanese mountain asceticism that combines elements of both Buddhism and Shintoism. En no Gyōja believed that mountains were sacred, and his journey to Fuji's summit was part of his spiritual quest for enlightenment.

As time went on, more and more people were drawn to Mount Fuji for both spiritual and personal reasons. By the 12th century, another famous figure, a monk named Matsudai, became one of the first recorded people to climb Fuji for religious purposes. His climb helped establish a long-standing tradition of pilgrimages to the mountain.

During the Edo period (1603–1868), climbing Mount Fuji became even more popular, with groups of pilgrims, known as Fuji-ko, forming to make the sacred ascent. These pilgrims believed that climbing Fuji brought them closer to the gods, and many would leave offerings at the shrines on the mountain.

While religious pilgrims were among the first explorers of Mount Fuji, it wasn't until later that Western adventurers and scientists began to take an interest in climbing the mountain. One of the most famous early foreign explorers to reach Fuji's summit was Sir Rutherford Alcock, the first British diplomat to Japan. In 1860, Alcock became the first non-Japanese person known to have climbed Mount Fuji. At the time, Japan had only recently opened its doors to the outside world after centuries of isolation, and Alcock's journey to the summit was seen as a bold and adventurous feat. His climb was not easy—he faced treacherous conditions and challenging terrain—but he was determined to reach the top. When he finally stood on Fuji's summit, he was rewarded with breathtaking views of the surrounding landscape. Alcock's account of his climb, published in his book *The Capital of the Tycoon*, inspired many other Western explorers to follow in his footsteps.

Another well-known explorer of Mount Fuji was Isabella Bird, a British travel writer and adventurer who journeyed through Japan in the late 19th century. Bird's travels took her to some of the most remote and rugged parts of Japan, and she was captivated by Mount Fuji's beauty. Though Bird did not climb to the summit, she wrote extensively about the mountain and its significance to the Japanese people. Her vivid descriptions of Fuji in her book *Unbeaten Tracks in Japan* helped introduce Western audiences to the majestic mountain, further fueling interest in exploring it.

As the 20th century approached, more and more adventurers, both Japanese and foreign, set their sights on climbing Mount Fuji. Among them was the famed Japanese mountaineer Yuko Maki. Though Maki is perhaps best known for his climbs of some of the world's tallest mountains, including those in the Swiss Alps, he had a deep admiration for Mount Fuji. Maki's passion for mountaineering and his expertise in climbing helped inspire a new generation of Japanese climbers to take on the challenge of Mount Fuji. His contributions to the world of mountaineering were recognized internationally, and he became a symbol of Japan's growing interest in modern mountaineering.

In addition to individual explorers, scientific expeditions to Mount Fuji became increasingly common in the 19th and 20th centuries. Geologists, botanists, and other scientists were drawn to the mountain, eager to study its unique environment. One such scientist was the German geologist Dr. Ferdinand von Richthofen, who conducted geological surveys of Mount Fuji in the late 1800s. Richthofen's research helped to deepen our understanding of Fuji's volcanic activity and geological history, providing valuable insights into how the mountain was formed and how it continues to evolve.

The exploration of Mount Fuji also became linked to Japan's efforts to modernize during the Meiji era (1868–1912). As Japan opened up to the world and began to embrace Western technology and ideas, many Japanese explorers sought to climb Mount Fuji as a symbol of national pride. Climbing Fuji became a way for the Japanese people to showcase their connection to their country's natural heritage while also demonstrating their mastery of modern techniques and equipment. During this time, mountaineering clubs were formed, and climbing Fuji became a popular activity for both men and women. By the early 20th century, Japan had a thriving community of mountaineers, many of whom saw climbing Fuji as a rite of passage.

One of the most notable explorers of Mount Fuji in the modern era was Junko Tabei, a Japanese mountaineer who became the first woman to reach the summit of Mount Everest in 1975. Tabei was born in 1939 in Fukushima, Japan, and developed a passion for climbing at an early age. Though she is best known for her historic Everest climb, Mount Fuji also played a significant role in her mountaineering career. Tabei's love for climbing began with hikes up smaller mountains in Japan, including Mount Fuji, and her determination to overcome challenges on Fuji's slopes helped shape her skills as a climber. Tabei's achievements were groundbreaking, not only for Japanese women but for women mountaineers around the world, and her legacy continues to inspire those who dream of conquering the world's tallest peaks.

The exploration of Mount Fuji is not limited to physical climbs. Over the years, artists, poets, and writers have also explored the mountain in their own way, capturing its beauty and significance through their work. The famous woodblock print artist Katsushika Hokusai, for example, created a series of prints known as *Thirty-Six Views of Mount Fuji*, which depicted the mountain from various angles and in different seasons. Hokusai's art helped to immortalize Fuji in Japanese culture and has inspired countless people to visit and explore the mountain for themselves.

Today, Mount Fuji remains one of the most popular climbing destinations in the world, attracting thousands of adventurers each year. Modern climbers benefit from well-maintained trails, mountain huts, and safety measures that make the journey to the summit more accessible than it was for the early explorers. However, the spirit of exploration remains the same, and those who reach the top of Mount Fuji are often rewarded with a sense of awe and accomplishment. The mountain continues to challenge and inspire those who dare to climb it, just as it did for the explorers of the past.

In conclusion, the famous explorers of Mount Fuji have left an indelible mark on the history of the mountain. From early religious pilgrims to daring Western adventurers and modern mountaineers, each explorer has contributed to our understanding of Fuji and its place in the world. Whether climbing for spiritual reasons, scientific research, or personal achievement, these explorers have helped to shape the legacy of Mount Fuji, making it a destination for adventurers, scholars, and nature lovers alike. As long as Mount Fuji stands tall, it will continue to beckon explorers to its slopes, offering both challenge and inspiration to all who seek to discover its secrets.

Chapter 18: The First People to Climb Mount Fuji

The story of the first people to climb Mount Fuji is a fascinating blend of history, myth, and spiritual devotion. Mount Fuji has been a sacred mountain in Japan for centuries, and the first climbers were not adventurers in the modern sense but rather pilgrims who believed the mountain to be a place of deep spiritual significance. Their ascents were motivated by faith, a connection to nature, and a desire to reach the heavens, as Mount Fuji has long been seen as a bridge between the human world and the divine.

The earliest known accounts of people climbing Mount Fuji come from ancient Japanese texts and folklore. One of the most well-known figures associated with early climbs of Mount Fuji is a legendary ascetic named En no Gyōja, who lived in the 7th century. En no Gyōja is considered the founder of Shugendō, a spiritual practice that combines elements of Buddhism, Shintoism, and mountain worship. He is often depicted as a hermit who lived in the mountains, seeking spiritual enlightenment through communion with nature. According to legend, En no Gyōja was one of the first to climb Mount Fuji, although historical evidence of his ascent is difficult to verify. His story, however, is an important part of the cultural and spiritual connection that early climbers had with the mountain.

For centuries, Mount Fuji was regarded as a sacred place, and its summit was thought to be the home of gods and spirits. As a result, it was not commonly climbed by ordinary people. Those who did climb it were often monks or followers of religious practices who viewed the mountain as a path to spiritual enlightenment. These early pilgrims believed that by reaching the summit, they could achieve a closer connection to the divine. The climb was seen as a form of penance, a way to purify oneself, and an opportunity to experience the divine presence of the mountain. Many pilgrims would stop at the numerous shrines and temples that dotted Fuji's slopes, offering prayers and performing rituals as they made their way upward.

One of the earliest recorded climbers of Mount Fuji was a monk named Matsudai, who lived during the 12th century. Matsudai is often credited with establishing the tradition of religious pilgrimages to the mountain. His climb, undertaken as an act of devotion, helped solidify Mount Fuji's status as a sacred site. Following in Matsudai's footsteps, more monks and religious figures began to make the journey to Fuji's summit, further embedding the mountain's spiritual importance in Japanese culture. These early climbers were not motivated by a sense of adventure or curiosity but rather by a deep belief in the spiritual power of the mountain.

The religious group known as the Fuji-ko played a significant role in promoting the tradition of climbing Mount Fuji. Fuji-ko was a sect of worshippers who believed in the sacredness of Mount Fuji and organized pilgrimages to its summit. The group was founded by a man named Hasegawa Kakugyo in the late 16th century. Hasegawa was a devout follower of mountain worship and believed that by climbing Fuji, one could attain spiritual purity and enlightenment. He spent many years on the mountain, meditating and practicing asceticism, and his teachings attracted followers who shared his belief in the spiritual power of Fuji. The Fuji-ko members would undertake pilgrimages to the mountain, often traveling from distant regions of Japan to reach its base. They would wear traditional white robes, symbolic of purity, and carry walking sticks, which they would use to help them on the steep and challenging climb.

During the Edo period (1603–1868), climbing Mount Fuji became increasingly popular, especially among commoners. The Fuji-ko sect helped make the climb accessible to people from all walks of life, not just monks and religious figures. Pilgrimages to Mount Fuji became a communal event, with groups of people traveling together to the mountain. These pilgrimages were not only spiritual journeys but also social events, where people could bond with others who shared their faith and devotion to Fuji. At the mountain's base, pilgrims would stop at the village of Yoshida, where they would visit the famous Fuji Sengen Shrine to offer prayers before beginning their ascent. The shrine, dedicated to the goddess Konohanasakuya-hime, who is believed to reside on Fuji, was an essential part of the pilgrimage experience.

Climbing Mount Fuji during this time was no easy task. The paths were rugged, and the weather conditions could be harsh, especially at higher elevations. Pilgrims had to contend with steep slopes, loose volcanic rocks, and thin air as they approached the summit. Despite these challenges, thousands of people made the journey each year, driven by their faith and determination. Many pilgrims believed that reaching the summit of Mount Fuji would bring them blessings and good fortune. They would leave offerings at the summit's shrine, such as coins or small tokens, as a way of giving thanks for their successful climb.

One of the first foreigners to climb Mount Fuji was Sir Rutherford Alcock, the British diplomat to Japan, who made the ascent in 1860. Alcock's climb was noteworthy because, at the time, Japan had only recently opened its doors to the outside world after centuries of isolation. Foreigners were still a rare sight in Japan, and Alcock's decision to climb Mount Fuji was seen as an adventurous and bold move. He documented his experience in his book *The Capital of the Tycoon*, providing one of the earliest accounts of a Western visitor climbing Fuji. Alcock's climb helped introduce Mount Fuji to a broader audience outside Japan, and his writings inspired other Western explorers to follow in his footsteps.

As Japan entered the modern era, the tradition of climbing Mount Fuji continued to evolve. While the first climbers were motivated by religious devotion, modern climbers are often driven by a sense of adventure, a desire to experience nature, or a personal challenge. Today, thousands of people from around the world climb Mount Fuji each year during the official climbing season, which runs from July to early September. The mountain has well-established trails and mountain huts where climbers can rest, making the ascent more accessible than it was in the past. However, the climb still requires stamina and determination, as the air becomes thinner and the terrain more challenging as one approaches the summit.

Even though modern climbers may not always be motivated by religious reasons, the spiritual significance of Mount Fuji remains strong. Many climbers still visit the shrines along the way and at the summit, continuing the tradition of offering prayers and seeking blessings. The climb is seen by many as a journey of self-discovery, a way to test one's limits, and an opportunity to connect with the natural world. The first people to climb Mount Fuji laid the foundation for this tradition, and their legacy lives on in the thousands of climbers who make the journey each year.

In conclusion, the first people to climb Mount Fuji were deeply connected to the mountain's spiritual significance. They were pilgrims seeking enlightenment, monks practicing asceticism, and religious followers who believed in the power of the mountain. Their climbs were acts of devotion, and their journeys helped establish Mount Fuji as one of Japan's most sacred sites. Over time, the tradition of climbing Fuji evolved, but the mountain's importance in Japanese culture has never diminished. Today, climbers from all over the world follow in the footsteps of those early pilgrims, experiencing the beauty and majesty of Mount Fuji while honoring the mountain's ancient legacy.

Chapter 19: How Mount Fuji Inspires Creativity

Mount Fuji has been a powerful source of inspiration for artists, poets, writers, and creators of all kinds for centuries. Its perfect conical shape, majestic presence, and deep cultural significance have made it a symbol of beauty, nature, and spirituality in Japan. The mountain stands tall on the horizon, its snow-capped peak reaching toward the sky, and this awe-inspiring sight has sparked the imaginations of countless individuals throughout history. Whether through paintings, poems, music, or even modern films and photography, Mount Fuji continues to inspire creativity in ways that transcend time and culture.

One of the most well-known ways Mount Fuji has inspired creativity is through traditional Japanese art. The mountain has been a central subject in ukiyo-e, a genre of Japanese woodblock prints that flourished during the Edo period (1603–1868). Perhaps the most famous depiction of Mount Fuji in art is the series of prints created by the artist Katsushika Hokusai, titled *Thirty-Six Views of Mount Fuji.* This iconic series features the mountain in various seasons, weather conditions, and perspectives, often framed by scenes of everyday life in Japan. The most renowned of these prints is *The Great Wave off Kanagawa*, which shows a massive wave about to crash, with Mount Fuji standing calmly in the background. The juxtaposition of the turbulent sea with the serene and unshakable mountain creates a striking contrast that has captivated viewers for generations. Hokusai's work not only showcased the beauty of Mount Fuji but also highlighted the mountain's role as a constant, unchanging presence in a world of impermanence.

Hokusai wasn't the only artist inspired by Fuji. Another ukiyo-e master, Utagawa Hiroshige, also created a series of prints depicting Mount Fuji. His works, such as *The Fifty-Three Stations of the Tokaido,* often featured the mountain as a backdrop to scenes of travelers journeying along the famous Tokaido road. In these prints, Mount Fuji serves as a reminder of the connection between nature and human life, as people pass by the mountain on their way to other destinations. The mountain's omnipresence in these works symbolizes how it is a part of everyday life in Japan, always there in the background, watching over the people and the land.

Beyond visual art, Mount Fuji has inspired poetry and literature for centuries. In ancient times, Fuji was celebrated in waka poetry, a form of traditional Japanese verse. One of the earliest mentions of Mount Fuji in poetry comes from *The Manyoshu*, Japan's oldest surviving collection of poetry, compiled in the 8th century. In these early poems, Fuji is often portrayed as a place of mystery and grandeur, its peak rising above the clouds and its slopes veiled in mist. The poets of the time were captivated by the mountain's beauty and majesty, and they used it as a metaphor for both the natural world and the emotions they experienced. Mount Fuji became a symbol of endurance, strength, and the passage of time, themes that resonated deeply with the people of Japan.

As Japan's culture evolved, so did the ways in which Mount Fuji was depicted in literature. In the Edo period, haiku poets like Matsuo Basho wrote about the mountain, capturing its essence in just a few lines. Basho's famous haiku, "Fuji's summit— / snow in a single spot / yet not melting," paints a vivid picture of the mountain in winter, its peak covered in snow that remains untouched by the sun. This simple yet powerful image reflects the mountain's enduring presence, unchanged by the forces of nature that surround it. Basho's haikus often focus on the idea of nature as a reflection of human emotions, and Mount Fuji, with its towering form and serene beauty, became a central symbol in this tradition.

In more modern times, Mount Fuji has continued to inspire writers and poets. The mountain has appeared in countless novels, short stories, and poems, both in Japan and abroad. In Yukio Mishima's novel *The Sound of Waves*, for example, the mountain serves as a symbol of purity and natural beauty, reflecting the innocence of the characters in the story. The image of Mount Fuji in literature often represents an idealized version of nature, untouched by the chaos of the world, and it continues to inspire writers to explore themes of beauty, spirituality, and the human connection to the natural world.

Mount Fuji's influence on creativity extends beyond traditional art forms. In the realm of music, the mountain has inspired compositions that capture its grandeur and tranquility. Classical Japanese music often reflects the rhythms of nature, and Mount Fuji, as a symbol of nature's majesty, has been the subject of many traditional songs and pieces. Modern composers, too, have been inspired by Fuji. For instance, Japanese composer Toru Takemitsu's works are known for their connection to nature, and Mount Fuji's beauty and spiritual significance have influenced the contemplative, atmospheric qualities of his music.

The mountain has also left its mark on modern creative mediums such as photography and film. The advent of photography allowed artists to capture Mount Fuji's breathtaking landscapes in ways that had never been possible before. Photographers flock to the mountain to capture its many moods—bathed in the soft pink light of sunrise, shrouded in clouds, or glowing under a full moon. The mountain's reflection in the nearby lakes, especially in Fuji's Five Lakes region, provides stunning opportunities for creative compositions that showcase the mountain's symmetry and beauty.

In cinema, Mount Fuji has been featured in both Japanese and international films. The mountain often appears as a symbol of Japan itself, representing the country's natural beauty and cultural heritage. In Akira Kurosawa's films, for example, Mount Fuji serves as a backdrop to dramatic events, symbolizing the endurance of nature in contrast to the fleeting struggles of the characters. The mountain's presence in films creates a sense of timelessness and awe, reinforcing its role as a symbol of something greater than human life.

Mount Fuji has also found its way into the world of modern fashion and design. The mountain's iconic shape and cultural significance have inspired everything from clothing to home décor. Japanese designers often incorporate images of Mount Fuji into their work, drawing on its status as a national symbol. The mountain's image can be found on everything from T-shirts and posters to ceramics and stationery, reflecting its role as a beloved and recognizable symbol of Japan. In recent years, Mount Fuji has even inspired street artists and graphic designers, who use its image in creative and unexpected ways, blending traditional and modern styles to create new forms of artistic expression.

Even beyond art and culture, Mount Fuji's presence is felt in the world of architecture. The mountain's perfect symmetry and natural beauty have influenced Japanese garden design, where the idea of "borrowing" scenery, or *shakkei*, involves incorporating natural landscapes like Mount Fuji into the layout of a garden. Many traditional Japanese gardens are designed with views of Mount Fuji in mind, creating a harmonious connection between the natural world and the carefully arranged plants, stones, and water features within the garden. This idea of balance and harmony, so central to Japanese aesthetics, is deeply tied to the presence of Mount Fuji.

Another way Mount Fuji has inspired creativity is through the practice of *bonsai*, the art of growing miniature trees in containers. Bonsai artists often shape their trees to resemble the natural landscapes of Japan, and Mount Fuji's iconic silhouette serves as an inspiration for the way these trees are pruned and styled. A bonsai tree shaped to resemble Mount Fuji might have a broad base and taper upward to a pointed peak, mimicking the mountain's famous shape. This connection between nature and art is central to bonsai, and Mount Fuji serves as a perfect model for artists striving to capture the essence of the natural world in miniature form.

In contemporary Japanese pop culture, Mount Fuji continues to be a source of inspiration. The mountain appears in anime, manga, and video games, often serving as a symbol of Japan's cultural identity. In these mediums, Fuji might be depicted as a mystical place, a location for epic battles, or a peaceful setting for characters to reflect on their journeys. The mountain's enduring presence in popular culture shows how it continues to inspire new generations of creators, offering them a timeless symbol to explore in their work.

Mount Fuji's power to inspire creativity stems not only from its physical beauty but also from the deep cultural and spiritual connections that people have with it. The mountain represents something far greater than just a geographical feature—it embodies the relationship between humanity and nature, the spiritual and the earthly, and the past and the present. Its image has been etched into the hearts and minds of people for centuries, and it continues to evoke feelings of awe, wonder, and reverence.

In conclusion, Mount Fuji's influence on creativity is vast and enduring. From ancient poetry and traditional woodblock prints to modern photography, music, and pop culture, the mountain's majestic form has inspired countless works of art. It has served as a muse for artists seeking to capture the beauty of nature, a symbol for poets exploring spiritual and emotional themes, and a backdrop for filmmakers and designers showcasing Japan's cultural heritage. Mount Fuji remains a source of boundless inspiration, reminding people of the power and beauty of the natural world and the endless possibilities for creativity it offers.

Chapter 20: Fun Facts About Mount Fuji and Beyond

Mount Fuji is not only Japan's tallest and most iconic mountain, but it's also a source of fascination for people all around the world. There are so many fun and interesting facts about this majestic peak, both in terms of its geography, history, and cultural significance. In this exploration of Mount Fuji and beyond, we will dive deep into some of the coolest and most surprising facts about this sacred mountain and the areas surrounding it. These facts will not only reveal unique aspects of the mountain but also extend into stories, traditions, and mysteries connected to Fuji and the regions nearby.

First, let's start with one of the most basic but amazing facts: Mount Fuji is actually a volcano! But it's not just any volcano—it's a stratovolcano, which means it is made up of layers of lava, ash, and rock. These layers were built up over thousands of years during various eruptions. The last time Mount Fuji erupted was in 1707, more than 300 years ago, during what is called the Hoei Eruption. Even though it hasn't erupted in a long time, scientists still consider it an active volcano. The idea that this peaceful-looking mountain could erupt again one day adds an air of mystery and excitement to Mount Fuji.

Mount Fuji's height is another fun fact. It stands at a towering 3,776 meters (12,389 feet), making it the tallest mountain in Japan. The height of the mountain is not just a static number—it actually changes slightly due to volcanic activity and even earthquakes that can shift the mountain a tiny bit. For example, the great earthquake of 2011 caused a very small adjustment to Fuji's height, though it was so tiny that it didn't really affect the overall measurement. Despite these minor changes, Mount Fuji has held its title as Japan's highest peak for a long time.

The mountain's nearly perfect cone shape is one of the reasons why it is so famous and so admired. Many volcanoes around the world have uneven or jagged shapes, but Fuji stands out because of how symmetrical and smooth its slopes are. This almost flawless shape has made it a favorite subject for artists and photographers. It is said that when you see Mount Fuji on a clear day, its symmetry is so perfect that it looks almost too good to be real, as if someone had drawn it by hand. That's why Fuji is often considered one of the most photogenic mountains in the world!

Another fun fact about Mount Fuji is that it is a very popular destination for hikers. Every year, around 300,000 people climb the mountain during the official climbing season, which is in the summer months of July and August. What makes this even more interesting is that the majority of these climbers are not professional mountaineers. People of all ages and fitness levels can be seen making their way to the summit. Some even climb overnight so they can reach the top just in time to see the sunrise, a magical moment that climbers often describe as unforgettable. In Japanese, this sunrise is called *Goraiko*, which means "arrival of light." It's considered a once-in-a-lifetime experience for many people, and the idea of watching the sun rise over the Land of the Rising Sun from the top of Mount Fuji makes it extra special.

If you're curious about how long it takes to climb Mount Fuji, here's a fun fact: depending on the trail you choose and your pace, the climb can take anywhere from 5 to 10 hours to reach the summit. Most climbers then take about 3 to 5 hours to descend. There are four main trails that lead to the top, and each one offers a different experience. Some are steeper, while others are more gradual, and the terrain can range from rocky to sandy. There are also mountain huts along the way where climbers can rest, grab a bite to eat, or even take a nap if they need a break during their ascent.

Mount Fuji is not just for hikers—it's also a UNESCO World Heritage site! In 2013, Fuji was recognized by UNESCO for its cultural significance rather than its natural beauty. The mountain has been a sacred place in Japan for centuries, and it has inspired countless works of art, poetry, and literature. This cultural importance is what led to its designation as a World Heritage site, highlighting not only its role in Japan's history but also its ongoing influence on Japanese identity and culture.

Speaking of culture, did you know that Mount Fuji is considered one of Japan's "Three Holy Mountains"? Along with Mount Tate and Mount Haku, Fuji has been regarded as sacred for centuries. In ancient times, people believed that gods and spirits lived on the mountain, and it was often a site of pilgrimage for those seeking spiritual enlightenment. To this day, there are numerous shrines on and around Mount Fuji, where people come to pray, give thanks, or ask for blessings. Some of these shrines are located near the base of the mountain, while others are at the summit itself, making the climb not just a physical challenge but also a spiritual journey for many.

Now, let's move beyond the mountain itself and explore the region around Mount Fuji. One of the most popular areas near the mountain is the Fuji Five Lakes region. This area, located to the north of Mount Fuji, is made up of—you guessed it—five beautiful lakes: Lake Kawaguchi, Lake Yamanaka, Lake Sai, Lake Shoji, and Lake Motosu. These lakes offer stunning views of the mountain, and they're a great place for outdoor activities like boating, fishing, or camping. On clear days, the reflection of Mount Fuji on the surface of the lakes creates a breathtaking mirror image, making it a favorite spot for photographers and nature lovers.

Another interesting fact about the region is that it's home to a mysterious forest known as Aokigahara, also called the Sea of Trees. This dense forest, located at the northwest base of Mount Fuji, is famous for its unusual landscape, with twisted trees and uneven ground formed by old lava flows. It's known as one of the quietest places in Japan because the thick canopy of trees blocks out the wind, and the porous lava rocks absorb sound. This eerie stillness has given Aokigahara a somewhat spooky reputation, and there are many legends and myths associated with the forest. Despite its reputation, the forest is also a popular destination for hikers and explorers looking to experience its unique beauty.

For those interested in more volcanic activity, another fun fact is that Mount Fuji isn't the only volcano in the region. In fact, Japan is part of the Pacific Ring of Fire, which is an area known for its frequent earthquakes and volcanic eruptions. There are several other volcanoes near Mount Fuji, though none are as famous or as large. These neighboring volcanoes, along with Fuji, help make the area one of the most geologically active places in the world.

Did you know that Mount Fuji has also played a role in space exploration? In 1966, Japan's first satellite, called *Osumi*, was launched into space, and Mount Fuji was used as a test site for some of the rocket's instruments. The mountain's high altitude and remote location made it an ideal place for conducting tests. This is just one example of how Fuji has been connected to technological advancements, even beyond its cultural significance.

In more modern times, Mount Fuji has become a symbol of Japan's resilience and unity. After the devastating earthquake and tsunami of 2011, Mount Fuji was often used as a symbol of hope and strength in the face of disaster. The mountain's ability to withstand the forces of nature and remain a constant presence in Japanese life has made it a powerful emblem of the country's endurance.

Mount Fuji has even inspired modern technology in ways you might not expect. For example, Japan's bullet trains, or *Shinkansen*, are designed to offer passengers a perfect view of the mountain as they travel from Tokyo to Kyoto. The trains are timed so that travelers can catch a glimpse of Fuji at just the right moment, and this has become one of the highlights of riding the bullet train. The sleek design of the trains, with their smooth, pointed fronts, has even been compared to the shape of Mount Fuji itself, showing how the mountain continues to influence modern design.

As we move beyond the region of Mount Fuji, its influence can be seen far and wide. The mountain has inspired people all over the world, not just in Japan. It has been featured in international films, television shows, and even video games, where it often represents the beauty and mystery of Japan. In fact, Mount Fuji has become such a well-known symbol that it's recognized by people who may have never even visited Japan. Its iconic shape and cultural significance have made it one of the most famous mountains in the world.

In conclusion, Mount Fuji is not just a mountain—it's a symbol of Japan's natural beauty, cultural heritage, and spiritual significance. From its perfect volcanic shape to the surrounding lakes and forests, from the people who climb it to the artists who depict it, Mount Fuji has captured the hearts and imaginations of people for centuries. Whether you're fascinated by its geological secrets, its role in Japanese history, or the fun facts about the area, there's always something new and exciting to discover about this incredible mountain and beyond.

Epilogue

As we reach the end of our journey through the wonders of Mount Fuji, we hope you've gained a new appreciation for Japan's sacred mountain. From its towering height and volcanic power to its rich cultural significance, Mount Fuji is truly one of the world's most remarkable natural landmarks.

We've explored its history, its role in art and religion, and the wildlife that thrives around its slopes. You've learned about the climbers who challenge themselves to reach the summit and the festivals that celebrate this mountain every year. But most importantly, you've discovered how Mount Fuji is more than just a mountain—it's a symbol of strength, beauty, and harmony with nature.

Whether you dream of visiting one day or simply enjoyed this adventure from afar, Mount Fuji will always stand tall in your imagination. Its snow-capped peak has inspired people for centuries, and now, it's a part of your story too.

Remember, the world is full of incredible places waiting to be explored. Just like Mount Fuji, each one has its own story, its own mysteries, and its own beauty. Keep your curiosity alive, and never stop exploring the wonders around you.

Thank you for joining us on this exciting adventure. Until next time—keep dreaming, keep discovering, and always keep climbing to new heights!

The End.